Why We Haven't Changed the World

Why We Haven't Changed the World

Peter E. Gillquist

Fleming H. Revell Company
Old Tappan, New Jersey

Library of Congress Cataloging in Publication Data

Gillquist, Peter E., date
  Why we haven't changed the world.

  Includes bibliographical references.
  1. Christian life—1960–   I. Title.
BV4501.2.G512   248.4   81-10580
ISBN 0-8007-1273-0   AACR2

For
Wendy, Gregg, Ginger
Terri, Heidi, Peter John

Contents

Preface

A man tends to preach his weaknesses. Of that, I am convinced.

My first book, *Love Is Now,* dealt with the love and forgiveness of God; I have always had a difficult time believing I was totally accepted by Jesus Christ. A later book, *Let's Quit Fighting About the Holy Spirit,* was written by one who had done his share of fighting over the work of the Third Person of the Holy Trinity.

This present work, *Why We Haven't Changed the World,* is likewise penned by one who tried in every way possible to see Christ's Great Commission fulfilled in his own lifetime. Only recently have I found the courage to admit that I not only have not done it, but that after my efforts had been counted, I was actually further behind than when I had begun. That is embarrassing.

I tried harder to reach new people than I did to look after those who listened in the first place. I was wrong. The hope for the unreached lay in the health of the already reached. I quit on the latter too soon. I have had to readjust.

And it all relates to being *holy people*—to getting our priorities straight—to putting first things first—and having the rest of what we are about fall into place. Read on—I think you will see what I mean.

The Old Testament's biblical texts in this book are from the King James Version, while the New King James Version, an excellent new contribution from Thomas Nelson Publishers, is quoted for the New Testament references.

Parts of three chapters have been taken from articles I have written, which were previously published in *Christianity Today, New Oxford Review,* and *Again.* My thanks to these publications, and to their editors Kenneth Kantzer, Dale Vree, and Weldon Hardenbrook, for the use of this material.

Of invaluable assistance in the writing and preparation of the manuscript were my cohorts in the episcopacy of the Evangelical Orthodox Church: J. Richard Ballew, Kenneth A. Berven, Jon E. Braun, Jack N. Sparks, and Gordon T. Walker. Thank you, brethren, for those long but pleasant hours around my dining-room table, and for the additional work you did at home. Linda Wallace captained the able "typing trust" of Doris Easbey, Shirley Dillon, and Bonnie Franzen. Steve and Amy Henne were extremely helpful eleventh-hour-reading critics. And Revell's Victor Oliver, though significantly older and more traditional than I, gave me precisely the on-target editorial guidance I needed. Thank you, and God bless you all.

Now may the God of Peace Himself
sanctify you completely; and may
your whole spirit, soul, and body
be preserved blameless at the coming
of our Lord Jesus Christ.

1 Thessalonians 5:23

Part I
A Frank Evaluation

1

That Haunting Vision!

During my senior year of college, I was confronted with the greatest challenge I have ever known: that challenge was a clear call to help change this dying world through global evangelism, winning men and women to Jesus Christ.

Without the slightest hesitation, I gave my life wholly and unreservedly to the fulfillment of that challenge. From that time on, this challenge—this goal—fueled my very existence. It determined my educational objectives and directed my vocational choices. The world needed to change. People in the world needed to change, and Jesus Christ could change the world by changing men. As I understood it, the only problem or consequence that needed to be surmounted was that of getting the message of Jesus Christ and His salvation to the untold millions, which I understood were as yet untold.

Aggressive personal evangelism was the bread and butter of my life for the next ten years. When I say aggressive, I mean *aggressive*. I talked with virtually everyone I met about how he or she could come to know Christ as I had. No one was likely to escape my eager witness: the attendant in the parking lot; the lady at the cash register in the supermarket; my fellow passenger on the plane; the student on the campus; the businessman in his office; the vacationer on the beach—I talked to them all. Hundreds and thousands of them. I assure you—I am not exaggerating.

Zealously, I explained the Good News of the Gospel the best way I knew how. I confidently and truthfully explained over and over again that people needed to experience a new birth in Christ, and following that, there must be solid growth into full Christian maturity. Furthermore, I shared the goal that moved me: changing the world by changing men through Christ. Many people joined that effort as the fruit of my encouragement.

A GROWING MOVEMENT

Nor was I alone. You will readily recall the growing movements of personal evangelism in this country during the sixties and seventies. You may have been part of one of them. Christians who had wished only in their most daring fantasies to be witnesses for Christ left the realm of fantasy, and plunged into the arena of aggressive personal witnessing. Whole churches rallied around great efforts in personal evangelism, some experiencing rather remarkable success and growth. Millions and millions of people were confronted with the Good News. There were many hundreds of thousands of recorded "decisions for Christ," and many were real and lasting.

Of course personal evangelism was not the whole effort by any measure. There was a phenomenal wave of mass evangelism, which had been rising in this country since the late forties and early fifties. The successes of Billy Graham, John Haggai, and many other evangelists fanned the flames of evangelism throughout all of Protestant Evangelicalism, and even penetrated into mainline Protestantism and Roman Catholicism. Evangelism was *in,* and it was producing results perhaps not known before in the modern world.

During the late sixties, however, I was constantly nagged by an unsettling realization that, though we were reaping an incredible harvest in terms of personal evangelism, our deep-down goal was not really being fulfilled. The goal that fired my imagination and gave me reason to exist was not evangelism, though I believed in it so much. My passion was to see the world *changed* for the good—for God. And it simply was not happening. There was no way I could stretch the truth to convince myself that it was.

The world was changing all right, but not for the better. It was getting clearly and distinctly worse.

The fact of the matter is, now in the early and mid-1980s, we are living in an era when evangelism in the Church has been prominent as it has not been, perhaps in the whole *history* of the Church. But—*but*—our contemporary world has continued on its own hellbound course at a rapidly increasing rate of speed, and with a more determined zeal than ever before.

You must not misunderstand. I am not now opposed to evangelism. I believe in it with all my heart, and I am still constantly speaking to people about Jesus Christ and salvation in Him. News of successful evangelistic crusades and the wonderful "war stories" from encounters in personal evangelism still stir me deeply.

Just the other day, a friend and I were playing racquetball. After three games, we headed for the sauna bath to relax before a shower. While we were enjoying the dry heat and visiting together, a college student walked into the sauna room to warm up before a handball game. He listened for a while and then he joined our conversation by asking, "What do you do for a living?"

I answered somewhat abruptly with the only comment that would come to my mind. "I work for the Kingdom of God," I replied. Even I was a bit shocked with the boldness of my answer— spontaneous and unrehearsed! My partner turned pale.

As I was beginning to fear what might be his wisecrack response to what could be rightly described as a smart-aleck answer on my part, this college student said, "Is that right! I've really been looking for God myself."

And with that surprise opening, the conversation turned to things of Christ, and by that evening, this honest and hungry young seeker committed his heart and life to the Lord Jesus. My friend is meeting with him each week, teaching him the Scriptures, involving him in the Body of Christ. Such experiences, I promise you, *never* get old!

A VACUUM OF RESULTS

But, I've had to face it. Our evangelistic enterprises in the late twentieth-century Church are not producing the change we all confidently predicted and expected. Yet that change *must* take place, if the world in which we live is to be significantly touched by Christ. Our evangelism has brought many decisions and some true conversions, but it has not even begun to slow the world down on its godless rush to inevitable self-destruction.

A while back, I was having dinner in Cincinnati with Charles Colson. During the course of the evening he remarked, "One of the toughest things I've had to deal with as one who is now a Christian is all this talk about spiritual awakening and renewal.

"In the last couple of years, I've set aside a significant amount of time in my schedule to study the great American revivals. Whereas all past awakenings had enormous effects on society and national morality, this one is just the opposite. Here we are, claiming forty or fifty million "born again" Christians in this country.

"But look at us. Crime is skyrocketing, murder is up, rape is way up. You've got millions of women having abortions. And now they're telling us about a whole new kind of dishonesty: computer crimes. True awakenings in the past changed the culture. This forces me to ask—is the current popularity of evangelicalism really a revival at all?"

Another curious dilemma facing us is the sensational rise of cults. Why, if the Gospel is being believed and preached as we claim it is, are these spurious groups growing and spreading in epidemic proportions? And, even more embarrassingly, "born again" Christians are jumping aboard these heretical movements as well. Whatever the cause or causes of this cancerous heterodoxy might be, we who promised that the spread of the Christian message would undercut such activity have egg on our faces.

I suspect the current failure rate among evangelical Christian marriages is not far behind that of the world. Two men who are both well-known evangelical leaders came up to me at a Christian conference recently to introduce me to their "new" wives. My heart hurts for them. I love these men—I've known them both for fifteen or twenty years. There was a murmur throughout the whole conference about the phenomenal number of divorces that had occurred, not only among the attendees this past year, but among the various leaders, teachers, pastors, authors, and evangelists of the evangelical movement.

After the last session, I was to take a cab back to the airport for a late flight, and a lady conferee asked if she could ride along. En route, we began talking about the marriage problems among today's Christians. I said to her, "Why do you think the divorce rate among us has gotten to such a peak?"

She said, "I really don't know. I'm divorced myself. Maybe we could have worked at it a little harder." And as we continued talking, I uncovered what appears to be a persistent and predictable pattern in these situations. She went through her problems all alone. Her church preached fidelity, but never intervened to help. We have been taught to make it on our own with God, and such individualism has not won the day.

WHERE DO WE BEGIN?

The solution to these problems is certainly not to forsake evangelism. And it won't do any good to sit back and take potshots—as too many do—at those who are really into modern methodological programs and strategies for world evangelism. Such useless exercises bring no changes, either.

There is a positive solution, however, and it will work. How often have we been challenged and excited by those assuring words Jesus spoke in the Sermon on the Mount: "You are the salt of the earth; but if the salt loses its flavor, how shall it be seasoned? It is then good for nothing but to be thrown out and trampled under foot by men" (Matthew 5:13).

There are two vital issues I want to comment on, using these words of the Lord Jesus Christ as my basis. First, the very idea of a people being the salt of the earth is staggering in its implications. Look, it doesn't take a lot of salt to change the taste and character of, say, pork and beans. Or, how much salt does it take to salt a quart of water? A pound? I should hope not! A cup? Still far too much. Why, it only takes a little salt to salt a whole pot of soup. That is precisely the way it should be with us who are the salt of the earth. We don't have to be a majority. Christians seldom find themselves a majority, except when they're at church activities (at least we hope they do there!). But it only takes a relatively few who are genuinely salty, and the earth will be salted. That's what Jesus told the few who worked for Him.

But this matter of being salty brings us to our second comment about Jesus' words. I am totally and completely persuaded that the reason our great endeavors in evangelism have produced so little change in our contemporary world is that we, the people of God, have lost our saltiness. We have relinquished our savor—that distinctive seasoning quality that brings good taste. It is the *Church* which has changed, and that for the worse. The world has merely followed our lead.

It is in the confidence that we can regain our saltiness that I write this book. The challenge to change the world still remains, but it will take more than new and grander methods of evangelism. It will take a Church that is truly and properly salty, a Church whose presence in the world will affect it as if it were being touched by the hand of God Almighty.

NARROWING THE PROBLEM

Two areas in particular present themselves where the Church of our time has lost its saltiness: *holiness* and *righteousness*. All the evangelism in the world from a Church that is not herself holy and righteous will not be worth a hill of beans in world-changing power.

Look at the context of Jesus' words in the Sermon on the Mount in Matthew 5–7. The whole sermon is about holiness and righteousness. Almost every serious Bible student recognizes that. It is here where we must change, and change we will—if we are willing to be what God desires. Holiness and righteousness may not be the only areas where Christians need to shore up, but I can assure you that if we can mend here, we will be well on the way to having the impact we must have in the world.

Religious action (be it personal witnessing, home Bible studies or mass crusades) apart from holiness and righteousness, is futile in effecting change in the world in which we live. A hasty glance at the programs of the religious liberals is all that's needed to confirm that fact. Over half a century ago, the liberals, seeing the ineffectiveness of evangelicals in effecting any significant change in society, launched out into social programming in the hopes of showing up evangelical impotence; but they did not fare even as well as we evangelicals. Their grandiose schemes of social reformation have generally turned out to be puny efforts, both because of the faulty theological basis of religious liberalism, and because, in my opinion, the designers themselves didn't have the true spiritual *oomph* necessary to get them off the ground. And even where there has been a measure of success, they have made not even the least significant dent in the hard wall the world has seemingly erected to keep itself from changing. It's the liberals themselves who accused the world of secularism and of bowing to a post-Christian era.

But listen—solutions *are* in order for the poor, the underprivileged. Some intelligent decisions must be made—and decisive action taken—to come to godly race relations. Social change is needed in many areas. But social changes themselves, even if ratified, don't change society. Such change must be accompanied by a powerful and genuine *spiritual* dynamic—a factor grossly lacking in current religious liberalism. The fact of the matter is, too many of the social changes being attempted now actually urge the world on towards its present demise. Social reform in and of itself does not equal change. It must come, instead, as the result of a fundamental change deep within the heart of a society. And it takes the action of a holy and righteous people to bring about the reforms that cut deeply at the cancer of injustice and suffering, and draw the world to its senses.

And the "moral majority"? Can't it change the world? First, let's hope the moral majority is indeed moral. It is one thing to espouse moral causes; it is another thing to live them. My greatest fear for the impact of the moral majority is that its efforts will fail, or even be counterproductive, if there is hypocrisy in the ranks. You cannot fool people when you champion morals in government, but still have not corrected the immorality within your own ranks. And I am not referring only to sexual immorality and divorce on demand among growing numbers of evangelical Christians. I refer as well to unchecked greed in business pursuits, covetousness in personal aggrandizement, and careless stewardship of resources among confessing Christians. People, the world is watching us! Our morality must be wholly characteristic of the true biblical morality, if we expect to really change our world.

It's patently not enough to talk about morality, and then excuse the lack of it in Christians with bumper stickers that remind the onlooking world that we are, after all, "not perfect, just forgiven." Judgment must begin once again with the household of God. It is we who first need to do the changing. God does not save us so we can just go on sinning. He saves us and calls us to be holy and righteous, and thus to be part of His purpose in reaching a fallen, bruised, and battered world.

ARE WE EXPECTING TOO MUCH?

Can the world be changed? Are the people of God even to expect such a thing? Isn't the world utterly and hopelessly lost? Why bother with it?

The world *can* be changed. The Church has changed the world before, and it can do it again. The impact of the ancient Church altered the character of the massive Roman empire. It didn't make it perfect, mind you. But it did make the world more bearable— a better place for both believer and unbeliever to live. Consider the issues of just treatment for slaves, care of unwanted children, the poor, widows, and the sick and lame, as a few examples of areas where the historic Church has made a visible and powerful difference.

The Church of New Testament times "turned the world upside down." And so did the Church in the centuries that followed. Throughout history, there has been a powerful impact on the world by the Church, sometimes great and sometimes less, but it has been there. Thus, our challenge today is not false, nor is it hopeless.

And we Christians *do* look forward to the Lord's return. Many of us pray regularly, *"Maranatha,"* or, "Even so, Lord Jesus, come quickly." But while we wait for our Lord to appear in all His glory with His holy angels, we must seek to do on this earth and in this world what God, who still loves the world, wants done. The instructions "Occupy until I come" have not been lifted. He is not through with mankind yet. The day will come when God terminates this age and brings a new heaven and a new earth, which He is preparing. But until then, we must treat the world in keeping with God's love for it. We not only may *expect* change, we must expect to *effect* change.

Holiness and righteousness are two indispensable ingredients necessary for the character and makeup of the Church, if she is to get her commission fulfilled. It is vanity to attempt the task without them. In fact, to pursue the task without them is not only ungodly, it introduces a narcoticlike spiritual fatigue into those who try—a fatigue that not only causes many to forsake the effort, but also to leave the entire vision, never to try again. Too many zealous Christians have burned out in evangelism, as they realized the results were in no way commensurate with the effort and cost put into it.

2

Is There Anything Holy Anymore?

Lest we become too despondent—and we must not be—about the condition of the Church in our time, it may be well to remind ourselves that in *every* age, in one form or another, holiness and righteousness have *always* been the two primary items the devil has sought to snatch from the people of God. Though they are being stolen from us in our day, historically we certainly are not alone.

Think back, quickly, to the exhortations of the ascended and reigning Christ to the Seven Churches of Asia Minor in the Revelation. Here we are, still in the first century, two generations away from the Son of Man living on the earth, and there is already need for warning. (Sin, by the way, comes *not* in being corrected. It occurs rather when correction comes and is rejected—or when correction comes, and you do not know you are apostate and thus do not hear. It is honestly that second category that I fear we may be in. Modern evangelicalism is, I think, in a modern Babylonian Captivity, and we do not yet know it.)

Ephesus had left its first love; Pergamum was caught in idolatry and immorality; Thyatira added to these same sins false teaching; Sardis left off from doing God's will and was found to be dead. Laodicea was lukewarm. Label it what you will, holiness and righteousness were lacking. And our Lord Jesus Christ came to His people through their leaders or "messengers" with a very basic solution: *Repent.* Stop it! Turn around. Follow, and obey Me once again.

Three centuries later, there were more vacuums of holiness and righteousness. The Church had made some incredible changes in the world. But once again her saltiness, and thus her influence, was beginning to wane. And as before, it was not just the people themselves who had strayed. It was the pastors or leaders as well—and it was concerning them that John Chrysostom, or "the Golden-Mouth" (called such for his ability to preach the Gospel), made his famous statement: *The road to hell is paved with the bones of errant priests!*

More recently, in eighteenth-century England, a group of students got together at Oxford University to try to bring an awareness of holiness and righteousness back into the Church. What they called for was return to normal, biblical godliness. Their number never exceeded two dozen, and the most famous among them were the Wesley brothers and George Whitefield. Their lives stood out in such contrast to the rest of the students, and to the society in general, that they were derisively named "The Holy Club." Not many of us have been tabbed with that label today, have we?

To illustrate what I'm after here, let's take the story of the rich young ruler and bring it up into the twentieth century. The encounter in this case is not between Christ and the youthful monarch, but between a modern Christian witness and, say, the ambitious young mayor of a midsized American city.

The Christian has just finished speaking at a fellowship breakfast at the downtown hotel. The mayor is in attendance. The theme of the talk was "A Purpose for Living." Afterwards, the mayor approaches the speaker.

"I really enjoyed what you had to say this morning."

"Thank you, sir," the speaker replies.

"Tell me," his honor continues, "just what does one have to do to receive Jesus Christ and know this purpose you have talked about?"

"Really, nothing," the speaker answers. "It's all been freely given."

"You mean, I won't have to change?"

"Look, you don't have to do a thing. Jesus did it all. You simply ask Him into your heart, and He takes things up from there."

The mayor closes in and says, "Look, what I'm saying is that I sometimes wonder about what I'm doing in my position. It's high-powered, you know. There are a lot of things, like the trips, the people—I honestly wonder whether I could really be a true Christian and continue in this—"

"Hey," the speaker interrupts. "The Good News of the Gospel is that there are no strings attached. Christ takes us 'as is.' And a man of your influence and your prominence—why, think of the scores of other young political leaders you can reach!"

"I'd never thought about it like that," the mayor muses.

"Here, let's step over to the side of the room, out of the way for a moment," the speaker says. "I want to ask you to pray this simple prayer. . . ."

That's scary, isn't it? On the one hand, it sounds so right, so *familiar*. In fact, you may have been on one or both ends of a conversation like that. But you go back and read Jesus' words to the ruler He talked with in Luke 18:18–27, and that account, and the one I have given, are light-years apart.

Why have we shifted? Has the world changed us? Are we not leaving *holiness* and *righteousness* out of the message?[1]

GETTING HANDLES ON OUR WORDS

Before we move on further, we must zero in on the two central words in this book: *holiness and righteousness*. On the one hand, it seems strange that they need definition. For many, perhaps they don't. But I have the feeling most of us need to have the terms sharpened in our focus, even though we've heard them many times over.

Holiness. To be holy means to be *consecrated, set apart, withdrawn from common use, separated unto God.* That surely is not an exhaustive definition, but it is a solid foundational meaning on which to build. Notice in this definition, nothing is said as such about *behavior*. Yes, behavior *does* relate to holiness, but you cannot start with behavior. If you do, you will not only miss the fundamental meaning of being holy, you will actually short-circuit holiness. Holiness begins with being withdrawn from common use, and being set apart to God uniquely for His glory, for His special use. Holiness is separatedness.

Looking at it from the back side, *un*holiness has been defined as being "profane" or not sacred. And the word *common* gives good content to unholiness. Commonness is the sense of not being special to God or not set apart for Him. In this context, *common* and *profane* mean essentially the same thing. So, being *made holy* is to be *set apart* from that which is common or profane—to be God's special property.

Recall that astonishing sight Moses turned aside to see, while he was out watching his father-in-law's flock. The biblical account of the burning bush gives us clear insight into holiness. The Lord spoke to Moses and said, "Draw not nigh hither: put off thy shoes from off thy feet, for the place whereon thou standest is holy ground" (Exodus 3:5). How is it the ground was *holy?* What made that bush different from any other bush? Simply that the ground and the bush were specifically inhabited by the Living God, set apart for His use.

Holiness for people is more easily understood if we begin by discussing holiness with respect to things, times, and places. If *things* can be holy, you and I can be, too! And if times and events can be shown to be sanctified, we have established yet another step toward grasping an even more comprehensive reality of holiness.

HOLY THINGS

Since things do not "behave," they are an excellent example that holiness is, fundamentally, being set apart to the Lord, and not a matter of conduct per se. Things aren't holy in and of themselves. That ground and that bush, which Moses saw, weren't holy before God came to meet Moses in that place. It was only when God set aside that ground and that bush for His own special use that they became so very holy. The ground and the bush ceased to be common and were now set apart for God; they were holy.

God takes many, many common things and makes them holy. If one were to make a list of the objects the Bible called holy, he would be quite amazed at both their number and the commonness of things that can be made holy. Consider some of the entries in your own Bible concordance:

holy nation	holy crown
holy place	holy ointment
holy kiss	holy oil
holy camp	holy coat
holy day	holy instruments
holy name	holy vessels
holy convocation	holy ark
holy habitation	holy offerings
holy garments	holy hill
holy city	holy promise
holy covenant	holy angels
holy ground	holy chambers
holy water	holy scriptures
holy calling	

Later on in the Book of Exodus, God spoke to Moses again about holy things. This time the subject concerned oil and utensils used in worship. After giving him a specific recipe which included the finest spices: myrrh, cinnamon, and cassia mixed with olive oil, God said to Moses, "And thou shall make it an oil of holy ointment, an ointment compound after the art of the apothecary: it shall be an holy anointing oil" (Exodus 30:25).

Why was this oil called holy? Because it was not used *commonly;* it was set aside to be used in the service of the Lord. In fact, someone could have stolen the formula, prepared the same mixture, and used the resulting oil to give back rubs or as a cosmetic lotion. Would this be called holy oil? Absolutely not. It's not only the formula; it is also the *use* that matters.

A bit later in that same chapter, God gives instructions for consecrating the utensils used in worship. He says, "And thou shalt sanctify them, that they may be most holy: whatsoever toucheth them shall be holy" (Exodus 30:29). This is not a table which will be used for entertaining, or the laver for holding the water for the family wash, for that would be common use. From this day forth, these utensils are set apart unto God.

In a similar way, the Old Testament tabernacle or temple where the Lord dwelled in all His glory became a holy building (*see also* Exodus 28:29; 2 Chronicles 35:5). And the seventh day of the week was called holy (Exodus 20:8–11) because the "sabbath day" was set apart for the Lord. Not just *another* building or *another* day; even time and location are made uncommon and are consecrated as God's day and His dwelling place. And the people were told to *keep* them holy.

Do you catch what is happening here with respect to *change?* Does God want the world changed? Yes. To what degree? As much as possible. To what extent? Everywhere! Including all these *things.* One of my problems early on in my Christian pursuits was that I had limited my vision for bringing change to only one arena: the hearts of men. Mark it well—God first wants our hearts, but He does not want *only* our hearts. He wants everything possible—"all things"—as the Scripture says, to be captured for Jesus Christ and changed.

I recall hearing a speaker years ago, who was giving an effective talk comparing Christianity and communism. One of his appealing one liners was "The difference between Marxism and the Gospel is

this: the Communist promises, 'We can put a new suit on that man';
Christianity promises, 'We can put a new man in that suit.' "

At first glance, we side completely with the second alternative.
But wait a moment! My Bible says it's both! To be sure, a new man
is infinitely more important than a new suit. But the good news is,
God wants to offer both. People and things alike are to be changed,
set apart to Him from common use.

Objects which are incapable of action are made holy. But so are
people, who think and act. The priests and Levites of the Old Testament were hallowed or sanctified by various rites of consecration.
Exodus, chapter 29, tells us not only of the consecration of the
priests, but also of their garments, the animal sacrifices, and the
altar—all of which are called holy. Even the things which touched
the altar became holy!

HOLY PEOPLE

Now, with these things in view, we come to that astounding exhortation found in both the Old and New Testaments: "Be *ye* holy
as I am holy" (*see* Leviticus 11:44, 45; *see also* 1 Peter 1:16). At first
glance, I tremble at the thought. Then I begin to grasp the fact that
if God can sanctify lavers, bulls, tables, tents, bushes, He can certainly set me apart for His use as well.

Isn't it usually on the matter of our personal righteousness that
the accuser comes and reminds us of our weaknesses? This is why
we must be sure we begin with being set apart to God as our *basis*
for righteousness. Then and only then will we deal with conduct.
And, further, we recall that Christ's strength is made perfect in our
weakness. Of course God takes weak people. Those who are strong
in and of themselves often do not even hear His call.

And, as God set apart people and property for Himself under the
Old Covenant, so does He as well under the New. For consider the
words of Paul in Ephesians 5:25–27.

> ... Christ ... loved the church and gave Himself for it, that He
> might *sanctify* and cleanse it with the washing of water by the
> word, that He might present it to Himself a glorious church, not
> having spot or wrinkle or any such thing, but that it should be
> *holy* and *without blemish* (italics mine).

Note the progression here. Christ sets apart His Church and,
withdrawing it from that which is common, He *sanctifies* or conse-

crates it for Himself. His bride is thus holy; she is Christ's unique possession. And she is *blameless*. To accomplish this, He withdraws us, His people, from common use and sets us apart to Himself. He makes us holy.

HOLY GOD

Of course, holiness of things and people rests solidly and solely on the fact that God is holy. Were this not true, no thing, no event, no person could be holy. For true holiness comes only from God.

So, when you think about God and what He is like, what is the first thing that comes to your mind? His love? His power? What about something like *heavenly* or *majestic?* All these are true about God, but when you think for very long about what makes God *God*, the thought that keeps coming to your mind over and over again is that God is *holy*. Holiness cannot be separated from divinity.

In the Lord's Prayer, Jesus taught us to pray, "Our Father [who art] in heaven, Hallowed [holy] be Your name. . . ." The angelic hosts praise the Triune God throughout eternity, singing, "Holy, holy, holy, is the Lord of hosts . . ." (Isaiah 6:3). The Trisagion (which means *thrice-holy*) Hymn, echoing this confession of the seraphim, is one of the earliest and best known anthems of the ancient Church:

> Holy God,
> Holy Mighty,
> Holy Immortal One,
> Have mercy on us.

Indeed, believers of all ages have everywhere ascribed holiness to the name of the Lord.

The Lord God, then, is in no way *common*. In fact, so separated is He from all that is common that anything common He touches becomes holy itself. And anything that will not become holy, He will not touch, for He has promised to destroy all that is unholy. Further, He is also holy in His perfect purity. Nothing profanes Him. No impurity is found in Him. He is holy and from Him all holiness comes.

Thus, by way of summary, holiness is *set-apartness to God*. And when we talk about "changing the world," we mean setting people and things apart from *common use* for God's use. All that is set apart to Him is holy; anything He touches or uses is holy; and anything He occupies or indwells is holy. It is this set-apartness to God which we must first have in His Church, if we are ever to make a positive dent on the world.

RIGHTEOUSNESS

Righteousness. A friend of mine used to define righteousness popularly as "right kind of living, God's way." That's not far from the center of the meaning for the word. Holiness describes set-apartness. Righteousness describes the *behavior* of holy people. Righteousness (or godliness) is uprightness in behavior. And that uprightness is measured by a specific standard: the perfection of God. If God is not in it, righteousness is called "filthy rags" (Isaiah 64:6).

For even as God is holy, so He is also righteousness. The manner in which God behaves is righteousness itself. Therefore, righteousness for people and things is determined by God. And happily He has removed the guesswork of the content of righteousness by giving us first the *Law,* then the *Prophets,* and finally, and above all else, the *Eternal Son of the Father* made flesh, our Lord Jesus Christ. For Christ *is* our righteousness, the One in whom all the righteousness demanded by the Law and promised by the Prophets is fulfilled.

As with holiness, *things* also have to do with righteousness. There is a right way for things to be used, and there are wrong ways. God sets the standard for what is right; men and their use of things are to follow it.

But it is to this question of the standard of righteousness that we must pay ever-so-close attention, in order to not be misled. How easy it is to allow the standard of uprightness to be set by others: our society, our friends, or even ourselves. Such disastrous deception precludes the possibility of true righteousness.

Years ago, in a small town, a telephone operator would receive a call each day from a gentleman at about quarter to twelve noon, asking the correct time. She faithfully told him, "It is 11:45."

One day, after several years had passed, she asked him, "Why is it you call me at this same hour every day to get the time?"

He said, "Well, I ring the town bell each noon. And I want to be sure I ring it right on time."

There was a long pause.

Then she replied, "Sir, I set my clock by that bell!"

If we take our cues for the standard of righteousness from what others do, gradually we'll be "out of sync" with the righteousness of God. Perhaps this is why righteousness is at such a low point in popularity and practice, even among the people of God today. Frankly, I purposely left the words *holy* and *righteous* off the title of this book. Bookstore owners told me repeatedly, "People won't want it." Face it: holiness is not a popular subject!

We've tended to measure ourselves—grade ourselves—in righteousness in relation to each other. Judging that God's standard is too unapproachable, we've settled for a pathetic, watered-down, pseudorighteousness of our own, and it has made both us and the world sick of it.

Righteousness relates to holiness as heat to fire. They aren't exactly the same thing. Neither are they separate. The one rests on the other for its existence. Holiness is the basis—that set-apartness to God; righteousness is the way that which is set apart to God behaves. Holiness is the fire which produces righteous heat.

MORE THAN JUST WORDS

So how do holiness and righteousness relate to the great need for a proper evangelism—an evangelism that not only gets right words out to a generation intent on destroying itself, but also changes it? Listen to the words of Peter in this regard, in 1 Peter 2:9,12:

> But you are a chosen generation, a royal priesthood, a holy nation, His own special people, that you may proclaim the praises of Him who has called you out of darkness into His marvelous light . . . , having your conduct honorable among the Gentiles, that when they speak against you as evildoers, they may, by your good works which they observe, glorify God in the day of visitation.

How clear Peter makes it that the Church of Jesus Christ has been set apart for God to do a job for Him. In the achieving of that task, we are to behave properly. If we will function in holiness and righteousness, we will be successful in our endeavor. *We can change the world.*

It's time to get back to these all-important components of Christian life. We must get them in sight and live by them in our daily walk, both personally, as individuals, and corporately, in the Church. I see several areas where spiritual smog with respect to these has brought a need for second- and third-stage alerts in the Body of Christ.

1. We have tended to reduce being holy to only behaving correctly, and that according to a human standard, rather than being set apart from commonness to God. To borrow a phrase, we have put the cart before the horse, and the reality of holiness is nullified. Thus, even serious Christians have "tried to be holy" and have failed. Consequently, the very word *holy* strikes a measure of fear (or even embarrassment) in the hearts of some believers.

2. In part as a result of the confusion as to what holiness is, we have stopped talking about purity in the Church. Many people who profess to be Christian are living their lives and forming their values far more in accordance with the way those who are *common* behave. As far as righteousness is concerned, let's admit it: we have lost our cutting edge.

3. We have substituted the tradition of men (Colossians 2:8) for the tradition of God (2 Thessalonians 2:15; 3:6). Thus, people find themselves being "holy unto men" rather than unto God, and are attempting to live up to rules which God never established. Many are stockpiling a spiritual credit rating composed of wood, hay, and stubble, failing to realize that what they are following is a largely human legalistic system, and not at all a path to true righteousness.

4. There is a dangerous division which has risen in the preaching of spirituality today. On the one hand, you will find pastors and teachers putting all their homiletical chips on the believers' security in Christ. On the other hand, the message in other quarters majors in the warnings of God and the fear of falling away.

The first can produce a sort of "I'm okay, you're okay" spirituality in which sin is either denied or dismissed; the second inevitably brings about horrible spiritual dysfunction and lack of confidence before God. Neither evokes true holiness and righteousness. The fact is, we must preach the totality of God's message: Jesus' promise that He will never leave us or forsake us, complemented by the admonition that we are called to endurance and the completion of the race.

5. Being Christians is often seen today as a purely individual walk with Christ, with little or no attention to the role of the Church in firm support and gracious discipline. This has produced an absolute disaster in terms of true holiness and righteousness.

6. People have forgotten *why* they are called to a life of righteousness. They think in terms of "being fulfilled" instead of obediently pleasing God, no matter what the cost or inconvenience.

In the pages that follow, we will look together into these basic areas, and into related matters, too. For we want to gain back both a solid understanding of what it is to be *set apart* to the Lord. And we yearn for a consistent experience of the righteousness, which comes through knowing and being energized by the Persons of the Father and the Son and the Holy Spirit.

3
Getting Motivated

Sweeping changes must take place in the heart of the Church before there will be any consequential change in the world. The Church needs to be changed first, before we take on the world! Holiness and righteousness are foundational to any and all of these changes, and these two characteristics of the people of God must come to mature reality with dispatch.

To be *holy,* as we have seen, means to be *set apart* unto God from that which is common and profane—to be used exclusively by Him and for His purpose. Through redemption in Jesus Christ we become His property; God removes us from ownership and use by that which is not under His domain.

To be *righteous* is to *behave* in a manner in keeping with God's standard, as those set apart for His use. Holiness and righteousness, it is true, cannot be separated, but there are distinctions between them, which we must grasp. For when holiness and righteousness are treated as totally synonymous, it is almost inevitable that deadly legalism will become the norm for Christian living. This is because proper behavior will soon come to be considered the cause of being set apart for His purpose. Instead, it is *because* we have been made holy by the Lord that we have the desire and the ability to live in a godly fashion.

But before we talk about *how* holy people live, in terms of the standards of and the power for righteousness, let us first consider *why* we are to live in a godly manner. Unless we have a proper motivation to live righteously, simply deciding to do so (or trying to do so), will not accomplish what we are after. Indeed, when proper religious behavior for its own sake (that's plain old legalism dressed respectably) becomes the vogue, the reality and impact of true holiness will be hopelessly lost. And the world will miss out on its salt and light.

THE MOTIVATION FOR RIGHTEOUSNESS

Perhaps it seems a bit silly to take a whole chapter to address Christian readers on the subject of *why* they should live holy and godly lives. The problem is, there have been so many humanistic reasons set forth to call us to good behavior, that it becomes necessary to review proper motivation for these from a biblical perspective.

We are not to live righteously first and foremost to please other people. That is not to say that godly behavior does not please others, for the Scriptures teach that "when a man's ways please the Lord, he maketh even his enemies to be at peace with him" (Proverbs 16:7). But our primary motive for godly living must never be to gain the applause of men. We are to live righteously for the Lord. *Period.* He is God, and He commands it.

Think of the heart-satisfying liberty which comes to a working man who realizes that working hard to please his boss—who may even be an unjust man—brings honor and glory to the God who set him apart to Himself. While the unholy are often "men pleasers," in Christ we are set apart from that kind of common behavior in order to be pleasing to the Lord.

And because we *are* holy people, we are actually capable of doing a better job out there in the world than we would were we not set apart to God. It is not that holy people get "smarter," but in Christ we are given soft hearts and renewed minds that bring increased wisdom, trustworthiness, honesty, and other fruits of righteousness. Then, as a result of living for the Lord, some of our fellow human beings will be most certainly pleased in the process.

The "peaceable fruit of righteousness" promised to the people of God is not *automatically* forthcoming. It is possible to stifle it. That is what is happening in so much of confessing Christendom today. Righteousness is more of a memory than it is a reality. Rather than a rich harvest of the fruits of holiness and righteousness, there is a scarcity of spiritual fruit in the Church, and spiritual famine is the result.

The other day, I was flying from Los Angeles to Pittsburgh. Seated beside me on the plane was a man my age who is an evangelical Christian and a psychologist. He mentioned to me his concern that we are rapidly losing godly behavior in the Body of

Christ. Then he made a comment which reflected almost a prophetic insight.

He said, "Ten or twelve years ago, most Christians I knew were
so bound up and legalistic, I found myself talking to them almost
exclusively about freedom in Christ. Today, just a decade or so
later, evangelicals are so licentious and self-seeking, I find myself
giving them boundaries from God's Word. I have concluded that
we must never divorce the righteousness of the Law from the freedom of the Gospel—and we have done it. Either one by itself is
meaningless and will lead to error."

The people of God must be willing to have the fruit of righteousness forthcoming in their lives. God will not force fruit through us
without our actively joining Him in the willing and doing of fruit
producing. Let me ask: Have you personally set your mind to obey
Him, to please Him, to be productive?

Next, we are not to live godly lives to please ourselves, that *we*
might be fulfilled. Here is where countless contemporary Christians
are confused. The idea that holy and righteous living is motivated
because it makes one's personal life happier and better cannot help
but result in self-righteousness—a self-righteousness, by the way,
which is a dangerous and false foundation for security with God.
Was this not precisely the case with the Pharisee in the Gospels who
thanked God that *his* self-righteous behavior made him unlike
other men? Remember, he—not the publican who prayed next to
him—went away unjustified. We come to Christ because He is our
Lord, and we live holy and righteous lives because we are accountable to Him.

THE FIRST WORD OF THE GOSPEL

This helps us to understand why the first word of the Gospel is
repent. We are called on the front end to renounce sin and turn to
Christ. The first account of Jesus preaching the Gospel, according
to Mark, begins with these words: "The time is fulfilled, and the
kingdom of God is at hand. Repent and believe in the gospel"
(Mark 1:15).

We surrender our lives to Christ because He is King. Some of us
may have genuinely come to Christ first, because He loves us, or
first, because He offers us pardon, or first, because He gives us peace
and a reason to live. That is certainly not wrong. But there is something even more basic to our receiving His grace. First and fore-

most, we are called to *repent,* to come to Christ because we are sinful and He is King.

Do you see the subtle difference here? This matter is critical, because knowing Jesus Christ as Lord and God is our *why* for holiness and righteousness. Those who truly repent—who renounce sin and selfishness—and submit in total accountability to God and His Word are those who become His faithful ones in His Church. They are used by Him to accomplish His purposes. Those whose primary motivation for following Christ continues to be getting their own needs met (knowing His power), and finding purpose and meaning in life, will face the same danger as Simon the sorcerer: self-gratification. We are called to forsake *all* and follow Him.

It reminds me of the story of a godly missionary who was sent out to preach the Gospel of Christ, to expand the borders of God's Kingdom. He was reporting back to his Church, telling the people what the Holy Spirit was doing, of people being converted, of the sick receiving care. He was so filled with the joy of the Lord, he could scarcely contain himself.

Afterwards, a young man, who had listened intently and with great admiration, came up to the older gentleman and thanked him for his encouraging report. He concluded his words of praise to the missionary by saying, "You know, I'd give the world to be like you."

The older man looked at him and answered, "Son, that's exactly what it cost me."

A person who wants to be made holy for what he or she can gain from the transaction has not really come face-to-face with Jesus Christ as Lord and God and King. If you have come to Christ only to have your life changed for your own benefit, I am calling you to move ahead from that place. For we are saved not for the benefit of others, not for the satisfaction of ourselves, but first and foremost, for God and His glory. And it is this biblical understanding of our salvation which motivates us to godly behavior.

With this in mind, let us turn to consider three proper motivations for Christians living holy and godly lives.

GOD IS HOLY

First, we are to be holy because God the Father, God the Son, and God the Holy Spirit are holy. As holy ones, saints unto God, we should live godly lives because we are set apart for, are loved by, and serve a holy God. This may sound basic because it *is!* Let's review God's holiness briefly, to make certain our foundations are properly set.

The heavenly Father is holy. In Luke 11:1, 2 Jesus' disciples asked Him, " '. . . Lord, teach us to pray, as John also taught his disciples.' And He said to them, 'When you pray say: Our Father in heaven, hallowed be Your name. . . .' " Our Lord wanted His disciples to be sharply conscious of the holiness of their Heavenly Father's name. So important is this that the very first request of this great prayer has to do with the holiness of the name *Father.* Certainly, God the Father doesn't need our prayers that He might be holy! He already is. But as the Father's children, our conduct reflects on His name. When we pray, "Hallowed be Your name," we are actually praying that to keep His name holy before the world, the Father will give us the strength, as His children, to be righteous.

Many of us were raised by concerned parents who understood the value of an honorable family name. Being identified with that name, and with the parents who gave it to us, we behaved in a manner which honored it. I have a friend who often asks his children what their last name is as they go out the door on their way to some special event. His children have been taught that whatever they do reflects on the family's name, either for the better or for the worse. It is *their* name, individually and collectively, and they are expected to use the honor of that name as a reference point for their conduct, wherever they are.

Similarly, as Christians, we bear the holy name of our heavenly Father and we behave in a godly manner because we are set apart to Him and desire to reflect well upon it.

One reason our Lord Jesus Christ came into this world was to make the name of His Father known. Consider the great high-priestly prayer on the night of His betrayal: "I have manifested Your name to the men whom You gave Me out of the world. . . . Holy Father, keep through Your name those whom You have given Me, that they may be one as We are" (John 17:6,11).

At least three consequences of the holiness (or hallowedness) of the name of God are evident in this prayer. From them we can gain a solid grip on what it means to hallow the Father's name. Physicians tell us that when a severely injured patient emerges from a coma, they first check the patient's memory by asking, "What is your name?" If the right answer comes forth, personal identity is secure to go on to other matters. Similarly, a Christian must know who *he* is based on who *God* is, and the Father's name is the starting point. Here is why:

1. *Christians are* kept *in the Father's holy name.* How crucial it is for us (whose safekeeping until the return of Christ rests in the Father's name) to behave before the world in a manner befitting that name. And how disgraceful to the Father when those whom He keeps in His name live like those who do not even know Him at all—even inviting taunts against the Father who keeps them!

2. Unity *of the Body of Christ is in the holy name of the Father, according to these words of Jesus' prayer.* Through being kept in the Father's name, the people of God experience being one even as the Father and the Son are one. Just as in a human family unity is in the father's name, so in the family of God does unity reside in our Heavenly Father's name. The name *Gillquist* gives unity to my sons and daughters. Even though they were born over a period of ten years, and consist of boys and girls, and have vastly different interests and capabilities, the name *Gillquist* unifies them. So we who are born into the family of God are kept together in the name of our Father, and His name gives unity to the whole family, even as that family is spread out over the ages.

In fact, to tell a tale out of class for a moment, I can think back to several occasions when one of my kids came to me complaining about another of our children, and the charge was "He [she] embarrassed me today at school." Why? Because of the instant identification of the common name! The neighbor kid can mouth off, and the effect is not the same. But let a brother or sister misbehave, and the family name is at stake. Father hears about it!

3. *Jesus made the holy name of the Father known so that the* love *of God might be displayed in our midst.* The Lord prayed, "And I have declared to them Your name, and will declare it, that the love with which You have loved Me may be in them, and I in them" (John 17:26). Everyone should know that love is part of godliness. Recall that the apostle John said, "God is love." Therefore, knowing the Father's name promotes love in the very midst of the Church.

Is any greater motivation needed for holy people to be godly than the honor and hallowing of the name that keeps us secure, gives us unity, and makes the love of God abound to us? Every time you pray, "Hallowed be Your name," let your heart be touched by the marvelous grace given to us by being set apart in the Father's holy name. If you do, you will be motivated to godliness.

God the Son is *holy*. It should come as no surprise to anyone that our Lord Jesus Christ is holy! Yet it is important for us to be reminded of that fact again and again, in order that we may be urged on to holiness and godliness ourselves.

The Son of God is holy because He is eternally born from the holy Father. He fully bears His Father's nature, and that includes holiness. This is exactly why He was able to reveal the Father to us when He took flesh and became a man. The apostle John put it this way: "And the Word became flesh and dwelt among us, and we beheld His glory, the glory as of the only begotten of the Father, full of grace and truth" (John 1:14).

It was the angel Gabriel who made the announcement to the Virgin Mary that her miraculously conceived child would be holy. It would be difficult, in fact, to find more holiness in a single Bible verse than in Gabriel's words of annunciation to Mary, "The Holy Spirit will come upon you, and the power of the Highest will overshadow you; therefore, also, that Holy One who is to be born will be called the Son of God" (Luke 1:35).

Those who truly know Jesus Christ know Him as the Holy One of God. And how could those redeemed by that Holy One ever consider living any way other than in keeping with His holiness? He is holy in His divinity, and He is holy in His humanity. We who share the new and glorious humanity which He bought with the price of His own blood must set our sights on holiness and righteousness because of Him, with Him, and for Him.

Let me say an additional word about the Holy Son of God. One day, as our Church Fathers at Nicea remind us, He will "come again to judge the living and the dead." Sometime, if you find your desire to live as a holy child of God slipping a notch or two, go back and reread Revelation, chapters 19 and 20. I want to say something as plainly as I know how to say it: *I fear the holy judgment of Jesus Christ on the last day.*

On the positive side, it is the love of God and my love for God which controls me and prods me on to righteousness. The Scriptures are clear on that. And His love is infinite, and holy. But on the other side of the ledger—at the other end of His holiness—is His wrath. I am accountable to our all-Holy Christ, not some lovey-dovey extraterrestrial "advisor." Secure as I am in His love, I still stand accountable to His judgment. Love and justice are *not* two separate biblical choices. Instead, they are two characteristics of the one and the same Lord Jesus Christ who has, in His holiness, paid for all our sins and called us to live righteously. Who among His saints would want it any other way?

God the Holy Spirit is *holy*. On the one hand I know this goes without saying; yet, on the other hand, it is so profitable to be reminded that the Holy Spirit *is* holy—*Holy* is not just His formal title.

The Holy Spirit bears the holiness of the Father, for He indeed "proceeds from the Father" (John 15:26). Since the Father is holy, the One proceeding from Him from all eternity has got to be holy. Thus, He is called the *Holy* Spirit. By this name we know Him, and by this name we are to become more intimately acquainted with Him. Further, in this name we receive the power and strength to fulfill our calling of being set apart to God by living in a godly manner.

On the Day of Pentecost, the Holy Spirit descended on the Church in order to lead her in the things of Christ. Together with the Father and the Son, He actively indwells the people of God. For this reason, Paul said, "If we live in the Spirit, let us also walk in the Spirit" (Galatians 5:25). The Set-Apart Spirit empowers set-apart people to live in a set-apart way. Therefore, if we walk in the Spirit, we will walk in holiness, living godly lives.

Our first reason, then, for personal godliness is that God is holy: Father, Son, Holy Spirit. Holiness is being set apart unto these three Divine Persons. Thus, we are to live in a godly manner because God is holy.

The next reason we are to be holy is not quite so familiar to us. It concerns not God, but *ourselves*. And we live in a time when the waters are somewhat muddied concerning our understanding of ourselves!

GOD DESIGNED US TO BE HOLY

When I was a young boy, my grandmother, who lived with us, had a big black umbrella (she called it a "bumbershoot"), which was kept in the hall closet. To this day, I have never seen anything that could repel the rain so effectively. It was so huge it almost enveloped me, as I would carry it during a storm. It would keep me completely dry from the knees up.

One weekend, a group of us went to the Saturday matinee to see a

World War II guns-and-airplanes movie. In one scene, a man parachuted from a B-21 bomber and landed safely in the bush terrain of Southern Europe.

Need I tell you the rest? Later than day I about *killed* myself when I hit the ground from the roof! And if I wasn't ruined, the bumbershoot certainly was. It could keep me from getting wet, but not from falling too fast from our rooftop. It was never *designed* to do that.

It follows, a *second* reason we behave in a godly way is that God created us to do so. By *divine design,* we were made to belong to Him and walk in obedience to His laws. If we misuse ourselves in sin, we crash—we are ruined. In his classic book *Mere Christianity,* C. S. Lewis tells us why.

> . . . moral rules are directions for running the human machine. Every moral rule is there to prevent a breakdown, or a strain, or a friction, in the running of that machine. That is why these rules at first seem to be constantly interfering with our natural inclinations. When you are being taught how to use any machine, the instructor keeps on saying, "No, don't do it like that," because, of course, there are all sorts of things that look all right and seem to you the natural way of treating the machine, but do not really work.

Not only was humanity made by God the Father and for Him, but He pursued us when through sin we strayed. He created us, and when we turned from Him, He came and brought us back. Thus, in that double sense, He is our *Creator* and *Redeemer.* We are not in any degree our own; we have been bought with the price of His Son.

In Hebrews 10:10, we discover that it was the sacrifice of Christ that established our sanctification, our set-apartness, our "holification." "By that will we have been sanctified through the offering of the body of Jesus Christ once for all." The word *sanctified* means to be made holy. Through His offering of Himself, we are removed from common use and made the property of God. We are made members of His Body, the Church, and no longer belong to ourselves.

Note in this passage, it is "we" who were set apart. The reference is to people—human beings—you. There is a crucial issue at stake here, and to miss it will impede greatly your ability to know the righteousness of Jesus Christ.

Occasionally, we hear teaching that only the human spirit can be set apart to God or inhabited by Him—as if there were some "spiritual" you that was both separate and distinct from the rest of you. No, it is *you*—all of you, everything you are—that is sanctified. As the Scriptures say, you become a "vessel for honor" (2 Timothy 2:21); your body is a "temple of the Holy Spirit" (1 Corinthians 6:19). Even the physical part of you is made for God, and His design is to set the whole you apart for Himself.

A DECEPTION CALLED DUALISM

The alternative to seeing the physical side of humanity as being "set apartable" is a cruel philosophy called *dualism*. Dualism is a tragic and deadly error, which is being unwittingly believed by some Christians. It is a system which sets some vague spiritual you against the physical or material you—a sort of good guy-bad guy war going on inside you. It's called *dualism* because it is a two-ism, where each part of you is a radically distinct power from the other. One of the "duals" is the spiritual or the unmaterial, and the other of the two is the material or the physical. This philosophy is false—destructive to the Christian faith.

Christians seldom struggle with the fact of God's being holy. That is self-evident. But when it comes to actually reckoning physical things in God's creation as holy—especially when that physical thing is our own body—that is something else again.

I'll state it plainly: Any Christian who believes his physical nature, including his body, is the enemy of his soul, will never experience true holiness. To believe such a thing is to believe a lie. I believe this deception called dualism has not only kept Christians from being all God wants us to be, but that *it has contributed to why we haven't changed the world.*

God doesn't sanctify some "spiritual" part of you, and let the rest of you go. He sets apart the *whole* you. If you will not accept, in simple faith, sanctification on His terms, you simply will not experience spiritual health and genuine righteousness. You will, instead, be your own worst enemy.

The danger of looking down on matter, the very physical stuff out of which we are built, has a long and unsavory history. Many of the ancient pagan philosophers were caught up in it, and their teaching has seriously tainted many others, right on down to our day.

In the times during which the New Testament was being written,

some people called *Gnostics* were tangled up in these dualistic ideas. They claimed to be followers of Christ, but they went so far as to boldly insist that the eternal Son of God did not take on true human flesh. Rather, they insisted He took on only the *appearance* of human flesh. Why? Because they considered physical matter evil. Therefore, in their scheme, a Son of God with a real body, which they considered necessarily evil, had to be explained away. So they did. But what they forgot was, a Savior who wasn't God in real flesh could not save real human beings.

Having treated the flesh of the Son of God so falsely, you can well imagine what these people did with the material part of the redeemed human person. They believed our bodies could never be anything but evil in this life. Following this disastrous error, they missed God's sanctification completely, and actually denied the physical blood that bought them. Salvation, in their way of thinking, was limited to a mental, invisible, nonmaterial *knowing* about Christ. As we would say today, they made faith in Jesus Christ purely a head trip. And their lives showed it. Disdain for the physical pitted body against spirit, and since the body was inherently evil and not really redeemable, you can imagine how they lived! God's purpose for them was utterly lost and their lives shipwrecked.

There are *not* two independent parts of you, a two-ism, a dualism. We do not have compartments, one spiritual and salvageable, the other physical and unsavable. You do have parts, but they are unified to make one whole you. Your body is His, your mind is His, your will, your human spirit, your feelings—they all belong to Him. Jesus Christ assumed everything we are—*all* of what it means to be human—so that we could be made whole and complete in Him.

At this point, you might protest, "But you don't know what I'm like. I have *experienced* being led astray by the lusts of the flesh." Here, one person may enumerate a stomach, an appetite that won't say no to food. A young man may speak of trying to "die" to sexual desires; yet another tells of problems in the area of thought life.

Here's the good news for you as best I can express it. Your enemy is not your stomach, nor your reproductive system, nor your brain. Your problem is *sin*. Remember, our Lord Jesus Christ fully inhabited human flesh. And He was tempted, in all points, as we are. But He never sinned.

Jesus Christ never condemned the appetite, nor did He condemn

sex, nor did He condemn the thought process. What He does say to us is *"Control them.* Bring them under My Lordship." Paul wrote, "And do not present your members as instruments of unrighteousness to sin, but present yourselves to God as being alive from the dead, and your members as instruments of righteousness to God" (Romans 6:13).

You are not your enemy; nor is your body your foe; nor your mind. Sin is an enemy; death is (it's the last one to be banished), and Satan is your enemy. Your salvation, your advocate, is Jesus Christ. The issue is, have you been set apart to Him? If so, to whom are you yielding your members? If you are giving them over to God, you will behave righteously. If you yield them to sin, you will be unrighteous. You do the choosing. And God has given you the power and the knowledge to make the proper choices.

The devil will lie to you and say, "You can't help it. You're stuck with an evil body, a bent and damaged soul. You can only be holy in your spirit."

But Christ has said to us, "You *can* help it! I have washed your body [Hebrews 10:22], I have restored your soul [Psalms 23:3]. Someday there will be a new resurrected and glorified you; for today I have redeemed you through My blood to live godly in this present age. As one I have set apart to My Father, brought into union with Me and empowered by the Holy Spirit, believe *Me*— you can say *no* to sin and *yes* to righteousness. I have made you, and everything you are—*holy."*

You, as a total person, are removed from the common and profane, run-of-the-mill existence to fulfill His great purpose for you. Believe it. Count on it. Act upon it. You will discover that you can live to the praise and glory of God.

GOD CALLS US TO RIGHTEOUSNESS

The third reason we live godly lives is because God calls us to do so. He is holy; He has designed us to be holy, He has now told us to be holy. Paul instructs us in Titus 2:11–13:

> For the grace of God that brings salvation has appeared to all men, teaching us that, denying ungodliness and worldly lusts, we should live soberly, righteously, and godly in the present age, looking for the blessed hope and the glorious appearing of our great God and Savior, Christ Jesus.

When God instructs His holy ones to live righteous lives, to behave in a godly manner, we need to know precisely what He has in
mind. For at this point it is so easy to substitute the commands of
men for the truth of God.

We have seen thus far that it is God who makes us holy by setting
us apart to Himself. Our holiness, then, depends on that which He,
in His mercy, has granted to us in removing us from that which is
common to be consecrated to Him. We have noted that godly behavior is an outgrowth of having been made holy, and that we are
motivated toward godliness because the Holy Trinity is righteous,
because people and things were created for God's own possession,
and because we are called to be godly.

There is really no reason the people of God should not have
their act together. God has done all that needs to be done on our
behalf. It is we who must now act in faith on what He has given us.
Some have counted holiness and righteousness too difficult, gone on
in sin, settling for commonness and sloppiness in living. Because of
this, the Church has suffered greatly, and so has the whole world
around. Others are intent upon obeying God's call to righteousness.
These are the agents of change. And exactly what that call is, the
content of what living in righteousness means, is the subject of "A
Primer on the Will of God," which is Appendix A in the back of the
book. These Ten Commandments are God's blueprint for righteousness for us. If you are a fairly new believer, I would suggest
that you read Appendix A before continuing. Otherwise, you may
choose to peruse Appendix A when you have finished reading the
book.

4

The Agony and the Ecstasy

There is an issue surrounding holiness that we sometimes prefer not to discuss. Do you want to be righteous? It will *cost* you. The Scriptures promise, "Yes, and all who desire to live godly in Christ Jesus will suffer persecution" (2 Timothy 3:12).

A TALE OF TWO KINGDOMS

Hear the parable of a kingdom, a usurper-prince of the realm of this world. By means of a masterful program of clever deception, he has managed to bring millions of subjects under his powerful rule. Granted, he has enticed them from the realm of another Monarch, but he considers them his. After all, they have been under his dominion for some considerable time now, and the Enemy hasn't yet taken them back. Yes, in the mind of this prince, these people are legally his people and this land *his* land. Possession is, after all, he says, nine-tenths of the law.

Suddenly, without much warning, the rival Government takes action. The Son of the Enemy Monarch is dispatched to the prince's very own turf (well, yes, he did steal it, but . . .) to take back those who would resubmit to His reign. The Monarch's plan is to draw these people out from under the prince's authority, philosophy, and life-style.

Most outrageous of all, the Monarch sets up His Government on the prince's own real estate. And instead of immediately removing His restored subjects from the country, He is keeping them there until a disease called *death* (a consequence of the prince's regime which eventually claims everyone) brings about a change in their state of existence. To make the matter even more aggravating, the Son even promises people that He will save them from death, and become the firstfruits by dying and coming back to life again Himself.

Unsettled, but undefeated (he thinks), the prince launches an all-fronts counterattack. Plainly, he is no match for the other King one on One. So he launches a renewed program of deception, simply lying to his citizens about the other Government. That doesn't always work, for the Monarch's Son keeps taking subjects back. Since they are such weak creatures, however, the prince sees no reason to give up hope for their eventual return. Consequently, even after they become citizens of that other Kingdom, he keeps the pressure on.

Falsehood is the prince's most common weapon. He uses it at the most strategic points. Since the most committed people are the most dangerous, he attacks the zealots among his former subjects by spreading rumors about them and intimidating them by hints of his power. By and large his successes are few, however, for these people demonstrate an almost supernatural attachment to the Enemy Monarch.

Still, the prince is encouraged by one relatively small, though nonetheless significant, source of help he had not counted on.

There are some servants of the Monarch's Son, mostly honest and well intentioned, who mis-state His promises. These servants are so intent upon winning people back from the realm of the evil prince, that they leave out of their messages some very important facts concerning responsible citizenship in that Domain. They rarely, if ever, mention warfare, or the prince's subversive devices, or the residual effects of the dread diseases caught under his reign. Frankly, they portray the Son's Government as sort of a spiritual welfare state, where there are free goodies for all, with little work or responsibility. One gets the picture of a sort of laid-back paradise, with the Monarch running a giant handout program.

Gleefully, the wicked prince capitalizes on this unexplained chink in their armor. All he has to do is let them preach these omissions, and then cash in on the contradictions the people experience in their daily lives. After all, his best source of returnees just might turn out to be the disappointed hearers who listen to these enthusiastic servants.

TWO SIDES OF THE GOOD NEWS

Realistically, the Good News has two sides to it: new life in Christ and warfare in this world. Never forget that! Our Lord told His disciples in Mark 10:29,30:

And Jesus answered and said, "Assuredly, I say to you, there is no one who has left house or brothers or sisters or father or mother or wife or children or lands, for My sake and the gospel's, who shall not receive a hundredfold now in this time—houses and brothers and sisters and mothers and children and lands, with persecutions—and in the age to come, eternal life."

This obviously does not mean that being holy in this life is pure agony. Not on your life! But being holy is not all ecstasy, either. On earth, the saints savor success but they also taste tribulation, though happily the end of it all is total bliss.

Now and again, we must go back and reread the passages of Scripture which we didn't underline, the truths we did not want to face up to. Most of us have passages we avoid or overlook, often almost unconsciously, because they threaten our private programs for personal spirituality. Throughout a wide swatch of Christendom, there is a concept called "Christian victory," which sorely needs a re-examination.

Too often, the "victory in Jesus" message is comparable to the halftime highlights on ABC's "Monday Night Football." They replay only the touchdowns and the long gainers. Rarely do we see the loss of yardage, broken patterns, dropped passes, penalties, or the painful injuries. In like manner, are we evangelicals not guilty of reporting primarily our spiritual highs, ignoring the exhaustion and pain, sleepless nights, hunger and thrist, cold and exposure, danger among false brethren (*see* 2 Corinthians, 11:26, 27)?

The "victorious Christian life" gospel is—at *best*—only half-true. Don't misunderstand: I do not believe for a moment that being in union with Christ in His Church is misery. It's glorious! But it is not flowery beds of ease. Our Lord said He did not come to bring peace, but a sword (Matthew 10:34), and a sword means war, and war means wounds and weariness.

Charles Swindoll writes to this very issue in *Three Steps Forward, Two Steps Back:* "Somebody needs to address 'the other side' of the Christian life. If for no other reason than to uphold reality, Christians need to be told that difficulty and pressure are par for the course. No amount of biblical input or deeper-life conferences or super-victory seminars will remove our human struggles. God promises no bubble of protection, no guaranteed release from calamity. Ask guys like Job or Joseph or Daniel or Paul."

If we expect a conflict-free walk with Jesus Christ, we will not be prepared to handle the inevitable trials, troubles, and tribulations which will confront us. Was it not our Lord Himself who promised, "in the world you will have tribulation" (John 16:33)? Fortunately, He did go on to say, "but be of good cheer, I have overcome the world." The Christian life is victory in the midst of warfare.

THE "PROMISED LAND" THEOLOGY

Think back through the "Promised Land" messages you have heard. Remember how bad they said the wilderness was? (All Israel had there was meals provided, cloud cover by day, firelight by night, and a God who, even in the midst of their rebellion, was "a father to them.") And recall how marvelous everything would be, once we crossed the river? "Everything will be all right, Brother. There will be glory on the other side." Somehow they never told us the price of the glory!

Consider just a small sampling of the problems Israel encountered after crossing the Jordan: the battle of Jericho; defeat at Ai; Achan in the camp; the capture of Gibeon; Azhor captured and burned; the gruesome and burdensome task of apportioning the land; the death of Joshua; Baal worship in the land; national apostasy; oppression by Amnon and later by the Philistines. All of this *before* the Book of Judges ends! Then comes the tumultuous Kingdom era and seventy years of the Babylonian Captivity.

There is no victory without conflict!

I once worked for a Christian leader who boldly proclaimed, "I have no problems." He was part of the Jesus-will-do-it-all-through-you crowd. But in spite of his optimism, he has lost three layers of his top leadership in ten years. Such an unreal view of life brings about enormous internal conflict in the lives of his associates.

God help us all to resist being regular-sized Christians making giant-sized claims. For spiritual life on this earth simply is not Eden extended. As British evangelical Michael Harper writes in *You are My Sons:* "We should not make the mistake of thinking that giving oneself to Jesus means moving the gear lever into neutral and coasting downhill, folding our hands and letting the Lord live His life through us. That is an irresponsible cop-out."

BEING SPIRIT-FILLED IS DANGEROUS!

Countless evangelicals are buying the "victorious life" theology, which tends to promise that once a person is filled with the Spirit, problems are alleviated—or at least greatly lessened. And the charismatic movement is riddled with a sort of "name it and claim it" bent, often accompanied by promises of material prosperity.

But when we allow the Book of Acts to speak to this matter of life in the Spirit, we get a far different picture. Alongside the ecstasy of the post-Pentecost miracles, you also find that Peter and John are arrested; Ananias and Sapphira fall over dead; Peter and the Apostles are jailed; Stephen is murdered and massive persecution of the Church follows; Simon the sorcerer causes great trouble; the Jews plot to kill Paul; Herod kills James; Paul is stoned; Paul and Silas are arrested at Philippi; riots erupt in Ephesus; Paul is mobbed in Jerusalem, accused before kings, and imprisoned; there is a great storm at sea and shipwreck at Malta. It is *in the midst of* these troubles and conflicts that the Church is victorious!

One of my heroes is Saint Athanasius. Under the authority of Bishop Alexander, he helped win a battle for the orthodox faith against the heretic Arius and his followers at the Council of Nicea in A.D. 325. But the war was not over simply because 318 bishops signed the document we know today as the Creed of Nicea. Subsequently, Athanasius was made bishop of Alexandria and was five times in exile, banished for a total of more than seventeen years. His life was in constant danger. It took decades to clean Arianism out of the churches. Was he not victorious? Yes, yes, a thousand times yes! But victory for this holy man of God came at grueling costs.

Or consider Dr. Martin Luther. His life was a constant battlefield. They called him, as we say today, "every name in the book." His adversary, John Eck, publicly dubbed him "heretical, erroneous, blasphemous, presumptuous, seditious, and offensive to pious ears." But we would not say it was all in vain. On his deathbed he exclaimed, "O my Heavenly Father, my eternal and everlasting God! Thou hast revealed to me Thy Son, our Lord Jesus Christ! I have preached him! I have confessed Him! I love Him and I worship Him as my dearest Savior and Redeemer! Into Thy hands I commit my spirit!"[2]

John Wesley is another saint we Christians in the West honor and venerate. We look back over two hundred years and see him as a model of piety and godliness. But the pain and agony Wesley endured was almost without parallel. On one occasion, one of his preachers, William Morgan, died following a long illness. Word spread that Wesley caused Morgan's death from excessive fasting which he, Wesley, had imposed. That false charge by his enemies brought great hostility, and people maligned him all the more. But Wesley was not defeated or cast down. We are told that at the end: "He died after a short illness in which he had great spiritual peace and joy, leaving as the result of his life-work 35,000 members and 54 itinerant preachers."

A NEW PASSIVITY

Our bogus notions of victory have made many of our Christian people unrealistic and passive. Christian victory has been somehow made synonymous with "living the good life." The smell of smoke and fire that adorned the robes of the ancients has all but disappeared from our vestments. We have been tamed. Have we not confused holiness with being "nice"?

Sister Mary Ann Walsh, writing in *U.S. Catholic* (October, 1979) charges Western Christendom with having undergone a "change in attitude which sees the Church militant softening into the Church hospitable."

Too many Bible believers of our day confuse "niceness" with goodness, choosing "gentle Jesus, meek and mild," over the Lord Jesus Christ calling the Pharisees hypocrites, and worse. Recently, some of our evangelical young turks have sat down at table with the Moonies at their East Coast seminary and complimented them on their sincerity and honesty. Egad! Have we no hair left on our chests? It's as though we want the final score in the conflict of the ages to be:

God—0
Satan—0

We have dropped back behind the lines of demarcation, and retreated to scrap with each other over spiritual gifts, submission, and authority—and Christian sex techniques. And we call ourselves a *Holy* Church?

THREE BUILT-IN ROADBLOCKS TO HOLINESS

In His Olivet Discourse, our Lord prophesied three particular influences that would present themselves to His saints in their pilgrimage to glory to get them off the track and turn them away from the faith. In the light of the battle that confronts us, let us consider this threefold warning, that we might be aware of these potential roadblocks, and thus deal with them vigorously when we confront them. Listen to His words in Matthew 24:10–12:

> And then many will be offended, betray one another, and hate one another. And many false prophets will rise and deceive many. And because lawlessness will abound, the love of many will grow cold.

Roadblock #1 is apostate Christians. By "apostate," I simply mean those who have left the faith. To help understand that, let me remind you that *apo* is a prefix meaning "outside of." State or status means "place" or "condition." To be *apostate,* then, is to literally be "out of it" with Christ and His Church. There are some very prominent, though sometimes subtle, forms of apostasy present in our day.

First is the immoral or rebellious "religious" person—the *licentious,* as the Scriptures put it. They live *outside* the Law of God. Even if these people continue in a "ministry," they tend to produce after their kind.

For years I was puzzled why so many of the converts of one prominent religious teacher were succumbing to immorality of every kind. Then one day this man's fellow elders announced they had excommunicated him for unrepentant adultery. He has since married for the third time—and is still out on the speaker's circuit teaching the Bible!

This is why the Scriptures set such incredibly high standards for deacons, elders, and bishops. Holy Christian leaders will produce holy Christian followers, but unholy leaders produce after their kind as well.

The apostle Paul reminds us that "he who is joined to the Lord is one spirit with Him" (1 Corinthians 6:17). Licentious people do not have the same spirit as the Lord. Since they are careless about their thoughts and lives, they are inundated by the daily attack of sin. Not having the mind of the Lord, not being faithful to Him, they value the "here and now" as more important than His Kingdom. Be warned, then, against following such leaders.

Another form of apostasy is legalism. Whereas the licentious step outside of and flaunt God's Law, living by the rule "everything's okay," the legalist *adds to* God's Law, imposing man-made rules as standards of righteousness. Instead of teaching modesty, for example, they prescribe dress. Rather than moderation, they teach abstention. Instead of wholesome discipline, they teach rigidity. Their legalism leads to rebellion, because wrong use of Law as a means of gaining righteousness always invites that response.

A curious, never-before-in-history type of apostasy facing us today is what I call "Churchless born-againism." This movement confesses a personal—really, *private*—relationship with Christ and denies the Lordship of Christ as being in the Church. Christ, they say, rules *only in one's heart,* and thus they end up despising God's ordained government. This view floods our modern parachurch movements.

Though many of the people in these Churchless movements are sincere, friendly, and gracious, they are tragically deceived. Unwittingly, by denying the Church and her various means of grace, they are producing, at best, homeless Christians, and thus massive apostasy. It's time we in the Church began interceding for these people, and calling them back home to Mother!

Roadblock #2 is the lure of false prophets—the preachers of heresy. The obvious ones are people like Sun Myung Moon and Moses David of our day and Mary Baker Glover Patterson Eddy and Charles Taze Russell of days gone by. But the ones tougher to spot are those out of evangelical and charismatic backgrounds who do a gradual shift from the historic doctrine and tradition of the Church. Watch out for false prophets whose hearts and minds have not yet been revealed!

Note carefully Paul's warning in Acts 20:28–30 that they will come from two sources:

> Therefore take heed to yourselves and to all the flock, over which the Holy Spirit has made you overseers, to shepherd the church of God which He purchased with His own blood. For I know this, that after my departure savage wolves will come in among you, not sparing the flock. Also from among yourselves men will rise up, speaking perverse things, to draw away disciples after themselves.

First, some come in from the outside. This is one reason God established shepherds over the flock: to keep the enemies of Christ *out.*

But how painful for Paul to have had to tell those Ephesian elders that "from among your own selves men will arise" to lead the people astray. False teachers also come from the *inside.*

All of us must guard our souls, and be obedient to the godly ones in authority over us, that *we* not lapse into being false, bogus believers. I beg you to keep your faith and trust in the Lord Jesus Christ pure and vital. Be sure your heart stays soft and pliable in God's hands. Turn away from pride, self-assertion, a desire to promote yourself. John Wesley once said he looked for people who "loved nothing but God, and hated nothing but sin." May we be so steadfast in our holiness.

Borrowing from the apostle Peter, we may say that there are three "tests" you can use in discerning false teachers, as noted in 2 Peter 2:1–3:

> But there were also false prophets among the people, even as there will be false teachers among you, who will secretly bring in destructive heresies, even denying the Lord who bought them, and bring on themselves swift destruction. And many will follow their destructive ways, because of whom the way of truth will be blasphemed. And by covetousness they will exploit you with deceptive words, whose judgment for a long time has not been idle, and their destruction does not slumber.

There is first the "Theology Test" (verse 1). It behooves every believer to know the basic doctrines of the Christian faith. Perhaps that is why the Nicene Creed is repeated every Sunday in most Christian churches. In it is embodied the central core of our faith. Those who come in teaching destructive heresies will eventually directly contradict or subvert one or more of the articles of this historic creed. There is, of course, much more you can learn about our precious faith, but the interpretations of Scripture set forth in this summary are vital. At the very least know and believe the Nicene Creed. And when its articles are violated, don't remain seated!

The "Popularity Test" (verse 2) cautions us to watch out for those with an inordinate number of personal followers. The apostle speaks of leaders who will be followed for their "sensuality." Again and again, we are warned by the Scriptures against leaders who pursue their own lusts and are licentious at heart. Anyone who willingly follows such a leader gets what he deserves, and if we permit such men to hold positions of leadership in the church, then because of our failure, "the way of truth will be blasphemed."

Then there is the "Vocabulary Test" (verse 3). A false teacher's program may be bogus promises or shrewd fabrications. He will make up a way of life and salvation which runs counter to that which God has established, and with it, he will lead people away from the worship of the Father, Son, and Holy Spirit. Pay close attention when you hear great and swelling words from autonomous religious leaders. An impressive vocabulary could be a dead giveaway!

Roadblock #3 to godliness is what Jesus called lawlessness. Like it or not, our environment *is* an influence on us. There is lawlessness in society, springing from that other kingdom. That is why there are so many warnings concerning our surroundings in the Scriptures. For instance in 2 Timothy 3:1–7 we read:

> But know this, that in the last days perilous times will come: For men will be lovers of themselves, lovers of money, boasters, proud, blasphemers, disobedient to parents, unthankful, unholy, unloving, unforgiving, slanderers, without self-control, brutal, despisers of good, traitors, headstrong, haughty, lovers of pleasure rather than lovers of God, having a form of godliness but denying its power. And from such people turn away! For of this sort are those who creep into households and make captives of gullible women loaded down with sins, led away by various lusts, always learning and never able to come to the knowledge of the truth.

In our union with Christ we have the power to turn away from the world's life-style, and reject this pervasive influence pulling us toward unrighteous lives. In our day, "lovers of themselves" and "unthankful" have come together to form in the world—and now in much of the Church—a spirit of antiauthority. It has become popular to be rebellious. In the world, Johnny Paycheck proudly sings, "You Can Take This Job and Shove It," while Hans Küng does the same kind of thing with biblical doctrine in Christendom.

We have become such a nation of self-lovers. Nothing is too sacred to leave—if we feel like it. We leave school if it gets boring or difficult; we leave home and parents if we're displeased; we leave our jobs, our marriages, and our churches. In the lawless spirit of this age the devil has become adept at enticing people to throw off righteousness and godliness.

In the context of the above Scripture, Paul implored Timothy to continue in the things he had learned—from the life and teaching of the apostle himself. Now, what Timothy had learned was to have faith in Christ Jesus, love God, and live a holy life. Popular or not, relevant to current philosophies or not, that is precisely our own call. For we are called to *righteousness,* not *relevance.*

FIGHT THE GOOD FIGHT

Do you want to help change the world? To do so, you must be committed to telling the full truth of the Gospel. Picking and choosing biblical passages to support a sugarcoated message will not do. You'll get large crowds on the front end, but empty chairs at the judgment. It is time for us to once again preach "all the counsel of God" (Acts 20:27).

All we have said here should highlight a certain unavoidable truth: We will not live "godly in Christ Jesus" (2 Timothy 3:12) without engaging in struggle and warfare. And though the warfare is against spiritual powers, there will be people on the side of evil, and we will have to fight them, too.

In the midst of this combat, we may be tempted to grow weary of well-doing, and give it up, to become "overcomers, retired." But the promise of the Lord is "He who overcomes shall inherit all things, and I will be His God and he shall be My son" (Revelation 21:7).

5
Crossing the Line

There is a curious difference between the ancient and the modern views of the Christian life. Today we emphasize the new birth; the ancients emphasized being faithful to the end. We moderns talk of wholeness and purposeful living; they spoke of the glories of the eternal Kingdom.

This is not to say the early saints ignored initial conversion; nor does it mean we today have forgotten about the eternal Kingdom. But our *emphasis* has shifted our attention from the completing of the Christian life to the beginning of it. Frances Eastwood, in the preface to her classic novel of a century ago, *Marcella of Rome,* says it well:

> As justification by faith may be said to be the key which opened to the middle ages the door of the Reformation, so the doctrine of the immortality of the soul, with its revelation of a glorious heaven awaiting those faithful to the end, was the grand point in Christianity which appealed most strongly to the feelings of the pagan, and answered most perfectly the cravings of his awakened spirit.[3]

The heroes of modern evangelicalism are the living, *contemporary* Christians: the famous authors, evangelists, Bible teachers, born-again athletes or politicians, who are in the public limelight with their stirring testimonies of dramatic conversion. But in days gone by, it was those who had *finished* the course, those who—living still, to be sure—had gone home to glory, who were counted as heroes of the faith.

The classic biblical passage describing how the early Church viewed its heroes is Hebrews 12:1–3. Note, as you read, the sense of the *presence* of both these mortals and their immortal Savior.

> Therefore, seeing we also are surrounded by so great a cloud of witnesses, let us lay aside every weight, and the sin which so eas-

ily ensnares us, and let us run with endurance the race that is set
before us, looking to Jesus, the author and finisher of our faith,
who for the joy that was set before Him endured the cross, despising the shame, and has sat down at the right hand of the
throne of God.

For consider Him who endured such hostility from sinners
against Himself, lest you become weary and discouraged in your
minds.

Notice, too, that there are no contemporary believers singled out
for the accolades of Hebrews chapter 11. Everyone in that august
assembly had completed the earthly pilgrimage in faithful holiness,
and had been enrolled in the halls of heaven. In the ancient Church,
no living persons were ever sainted. This is not to say that living
Christians are not saints: the Scriptures call them such. It is necessary to point out that the early Christians designated their godly
heroes only from the ranks of those who had *finished* the journey
successfully. Simply starting well with the Lord was not enough.

We begin to get a message here, do we not? *Remaining* faithful to
Christ is essential to true holiness, and is of eternal importance in
His sight. It is not adequate merely to have a spectacular conversion
or a glowing story of deliverance. God calls us to be on our feet and
in the fight at the final bell.

There is a great danger, in fact, about sainting people—excitedly
designating them as "gifted Christian leaders" or "great men of
God"—too early. We have made our heroes the *starters,* not the
finishers!

How much safer it is for us to hold the saints and martyrs of
Christ from days gone by in proper high esteem, to read of their
faith and tell their stories to our children, realizing that all the votes
are not yet in for those of us who are still in our pilgrimage to the
City of God.

In this chapter, I want to focus our attention on the aspect of holiness which has to do with committing ourselves to *finishing* the
race that Christ has placed us in. Holiness is not static; it is ongoing,
dynamic, growing.

FINISHING THE RACE

In my sixteenth year I learned a lesson that has somehow stayed with me until today.

I had gone out for the high-school cross-country team—a sport that to this day I consider the absolutely worst way in all the world to earn an athletic letter! It was the first day of practice, and the coach had taken us on the bus to a course that ran up and down several hills over a four-mile span. For those of us who were not in good shape, or who had never run distance races before, the prospects of that late afternoon were particularly dismal.

Before he fired the starting gun, that coach said something to us that I have never forgotten. "What I am asking you to do today is to finish the race. If you don't plan to finish, then I do not want you to start. Simply stay where you are when the gun is fired. But if you start, then you *will* finish. Remember, should your legs tighten, or your stomach cramp, you may slow down or even stop for a bit. But you will not quit once you have begun. We'll wait here all night if need be. If you agree to start, then I want you to cross this finish line—no matter what."

The first mile was almost euphoric. The cool, fresh autumn air was a natural boost to my dogged determination to run a good race. But after a mile and a half or so, the joy began to fade. By two miles, whatever pleasure there had been in all of this was totally gone. From here on out, it was sheer drudgery. Some of my teammates were depositing the egg-salad sandwiches they had eaten that noon at the school cafeteria in the tall grass and bushes at the edge of the course. They would stop for a bit, find some relief, and then fall back into the panting procession.

My legs started to cramp. I did not know thigh muscles could ever be so tired. And I felt that my breath would leave me forever; my lungs and chest cavity were in almost unbearable pain, as I approached the enormous upward hill near the two-and-one-half-mile mark.

There was one thing and one thing only that kept me going. *Before I started, I had agreed to finish the race.* My body said, *Quit!* My mind silently screamed, *Insanity!* But the choice had been made way back there, when the gun went off. That issue was not open for renegotiation. There were no options, no shortcuts. In inexpressible agony, I kept on running.

I can barely remember crossing the finish line. They said I came in fifth or sixth. But even that was not of first importance. Every ounce of energy I knew had gone into crossing that line. I really could not believe I had made it.

We must have waited around thirty or forty minutes for the rest of the team to finish. It was dark and bitterly cold by the time the last man crossed the line—but everyone was accounted for. We caught our breath, grumbled a bit, and then boarded the bus for home.

Over the years, I have thought back to that experience as being an incredible picture of what it is to live the Christian life. In fact, the Scriptures more than once use the metaphor of our life with Christ being a race. And it's not a sprint, mind you, it's a marathon.

In any race there are three basic and essential components: *the start, the race itself,* and *the finish.* And you need all three to win. You can have the fastest exit from the starting blocks known to man, but if you are slow on the turn, or sloppy in the stretch, your record start will not be sufficient for victory. Or, you can be unbeatable on the open track, but if you drop out fifty yards short of the goal, the rest of the effort is for naught. In any race, it's the first runner *across the line* who wins.

Most of all, however, be it in athletics or be it in the Christian journey, you must finish the race in order to qualify for the final count. Dropouts will never be world-changers. There will be varying degrees of speed and ability. But when we are set apart unto the Lord, His goal for us is to finish. Starting and running the race are the vital, but incomplete, means to the end.

STARTING BLOCKS

For the Christian, the start of our faith is the *new birth.* We come to Christ by faith and in Holy Baptism are placed into union with Him. For Jesus said, "Most assuredly, I say to you, unless one is born of water and the Spirit, he cannot enter the Kingdom of God" (John 3:5).

We have to remember that saving faith is the all-important beginning of our life in Christ, but that we do not *stop* with faith. Paul writes, "Therefore, having been justified by faith, we have peace with God through our Lord Jesus Christ, through whom also we have *access by faith* into this grace in which we stand, and rejoice in hope of the glory of God" (Romans 5:1, 2, italics mine). The New American Standard Bible uses the word *introduction* for "access" here.

I am troubled by the unbalanced emphasis today on getting people to make a one-time "decision for Christ." Don't get me wrong: I call people to make decisions for Christ almost every time I speak. But the implication so often is, simply saying yes once will, in and of itself, see you through.

Let us be clear on this. You cannot even qualify for the Christian race, unless you place your faith in Him. But the goal is not reached by a *one-time* response to Christ. No, finishing the race requires perseverance down to the wire: "For we have become partakers of Christ if we hold the beginning of our confidence steadfast to the end" (Hebrews 3:14).

In our era, the major thrust has been on getting people to make an initial turn to Christ. It is hard to object to any attempt to get people to put their trust in Him. But I will say plainly, God is sick and tired of people who call for first-time "decisions" but are not committed enough to make sure those who respond go on with God in His Church. Jesus told us to make disciples, not to get decisions. If disciples are not the goal, we are only cluttering up the track!

There is nothing cuter than a six-month-old baby. It is at this stage that an infant develops eye contact, the cooing stage is underway, and generally the little person has learned to sleep all night. But, if that is all the maturity the person has shown at fifteen years of age, it is no longer cute. It is tragic. Let's have all the legitimate new births we can get. But let us be sure they are born again into a household—the Church of God—where growth occurs and where the holy ones are called upon to complete the race set before them.

A five-run first inning, an eighty-yard opening kickoff return for a score are fine. Bring them on. But let us keep in mind that the real issue, the ultimate goal, is—did we bring the game to victory at the end? An effective beginning is only as good as an effectual ending.

THE LONG STRETCH

We are made holy, we are set apart from commonality for God's use, in order to enter the race. By the power of the Holy Spirit, we run the course set before us. And how crucial it is for us, as we are running, to keep our eyes fastened on ". . . the prize of the upward call of God in Christ Jesus" (Philippians 3:14). We must resist the temptation of thinking that just because we have made a good start, victory is automatic and quitting impossible. The warning Paul issued to the first-century Galatians comes through to us moderns as well. "You ran well. Who hindered you from obeying the truth?" (Galatians 5:7).

In 1 Corinthians 9:24–27, the apostle again uses the theme of a race as a picture of the Christian life. And what a challenge he issues to the holy ones of God. He writes:

> Do you not know that those who run in a race all run, but one receives the prize? Run in such a way that you may obtain it. And everyone who competes for the prize is temperate in all things. Now they do it to obtain a perishable crown, but we an imperishable.

> Therefore I run thus: not with uncertainty. Thus I fight: not as one who beats the air. But I discipline my body and bring it into subjection, lest, when I have preached to others, I myself should become disqualified.

Note first, that everyone is to run to win. All do not finish in first place, but we are all to run with winning in mind. Obviously, Paul is not saying only one, the first-place finisher, will make it on to heaven. But it is an eternal mistake for any of us to assess our own abilities, and then shoot to finish second, or third, or fourth. Do not become complacent or determine, "Well, I have only a few talents"; or "The Lord made me a 'thirtyfold' Christian." It's God's business to determine our capabilities, not ours! Thus, we do not second-guess our spiritual equipping, and run accordingly. Instead, we always run to finish first.

Though the ultimate and eternal prize is that for which we strive, we do not look down the long course of life and see *nothing* else for which to strive. No runner in a long race thinks only about the finish line. He looks ahead to a familiar landmark, a tree, the peak of a hill, a bridge, and determines to reach that point. Similarly, the apostle Paul, in his letter to the Philippians, tells that he is ". . . reaching forward to those things which are ahead," and pressing "toward the goal for the prize . . ." (3:13, 14). He isn't trying to make it all the way in one big gulp!

In a certain sense, it is always "one day at a time," although there are many landmarks visible up ahead. And notice, I said *ahead.*

Old age has been described as that time of life in which a person looks backward, not forward. But though there are memories, a life consecrated to God is one which looks forward—to trials which must be faced, tasks which must be completed, challenges to be met, and worship to be enacted. If we can think of nothing else, there are always evening or morning prayers, the next Sunday's worship, the coming Advent, Lent, Easter or Pentecost toward which to look. We persevere in the tasks at hand until that next landmark is reached, and then we fix our eyes upon the one which follows.

Nor do I discount the value to our human hearts of the anticipation of lesser (but still very important) goals, such as the birth of a child and that child's growth to maturity; family reunions and the enjoyment of familiar faces; or the achievement of well-deserved vocational goals. All of these are also holy landmarks in the lives of people who are abandoned to God.

The biblical phrase "walk in the Spirit" is helpful here. A literal rendering is "lock step with" the Holy Spirit—"fall into step" with Him. It is as though the Holy Spirit is calling out a heavenly cadence—*left,* right, *left,* right, *one,* two, *one,* two—to the Church. Those who are born of God and have the Holy Spirit are given ears to hear the commands of God and new hearts to obey them and carry them out. But we also are given eyes to see where our predecessors have gone. Their stories of faith, the Scriptures tell us, have been written for our instruction. As those set apart to God, we keep step, not with the world, but with the Holy Spirit who speaks to the Church. The crown of victory for such persistent obedience is imperishable.

A final observation on Paul's exhortation to the Corinthians has to do with his own personal concern regarding himself. To me, this is one of the most sobering passages in all of Scripture. For in his steadfast aim to run well in the long stretch of his earthly Christian pilgrimage, he does not discount the possibility that ". . . when I have preached to others, I myself should be disqualified" (1 Corinthians 9:27). If the same one who writes, "For I am persuaded that neither death nor life, nor angels nor principalities nor powers, nor things present nor things to come, nor height nor depth, nor any other created thing, shall be able to separate us from the love of God which is in Christ Jesus our Lord" (Romans 8:38, 39) gives this warning, we need to listen all the more carefully.

Many of us in contemporary evangelicalism have paid nearly exclusive attention to the believers' security passages, *and they are there*. But we have virtually ignored the passages of God's explicit warnings against apostasy, and *they* are there! We had better hear both the promise of glory and the warning of judgment. The fact is, if I quit the race in mid-life, I will be disqualified. I cannot get around that truth in the Scripture.

And rather than sitting around arguing the point, or trying to figure out everything inherent in the meaning of *disqualify,* we Christians had better get on with this business of living as holy people, staying on track and finishing the race which is set before us. If Paul didn't become enamored with his past services and faithfulness to the Lord, then by all means neither should we.

CROSSING THE LINE

If the starting point of holiness is the new birth, if the race itself is to walk in the Spirit, the finish line is the "crown of life" (James 1:12). It's those three absolutely necessary elements again: the start, the race to be run well, and the finish. Like our predecessors in Christ, we recognize all three.

Choosing one or even two of these elements as a point of emphasis will invariably open the door to unholy conduct and imbalanced faith. This race is not positional, not mental, not symbolic. It is as real as life itself! You and I are set apart to God for the purpose of *running to win* and *crossing the line at the end.*

Is this attainable? Of course it is. Do not forget: through faith, you have come into living union with the One who is Author and Perfector (Finisher) of the race. Our Lord Jesus Christ not only conceived of and designed the course we run in His Church, but in His humanity, He completed it and gives us His strength to do the same. We take part in His mission. When He prayed, "I have glorified You on the earth. I have finished the work which You have given Me to do" (John 17:4), He stood before His Father as victor in the battle. It is *in His victory* that we enter the competition ourselves. The One from whom we draw our life is already in the winner's circle.

In the last New Testament letter written by Paul, he acknowledges to Timothy that he has completed the race, in 2 Timothy 4:7, 8:

I have fought the good fight, I have finished the race, I have kept the faith. Finally, there is laid up for me the crown of righteousness, which the Lord, the righteous Judge, will give me on that Day; and not to me only, but also to all who have loved His appearing.

In an era when holiness has become a forgotten theme, the Christian life is sometimes described as a "party," a "dance," or as a prosperity-oriented, problem-free "abundant life." But Paul, who had been set apart unto God, who knew the raging battle of Kingdom against kingdom, called his pilgrimage with Christ a "good fight." Doesn't that say it? It is *good* because of the One who has called us to win; it's a *fight* because we constantly war and battle against the enemy.

Paul not only engaged in the battle—he not only ran the race—he completed it. The one who possessed a holy, healthy fear that he might not finish, *finished!* It was just a short time after his final correspondence to his beloved understudy Timothy that this great Apostle to the Gentiles was martyred in Rome and received the very crown of righteousness of which he wrote.

Of all the things in the Kingdom of God I want to experience, none surpasses the goal of crossing the finish line, being brought before the throne of God, face-to-face with the Shepherd of my soul, our great heavenly Bishop, and hearing Him say, "Well done thou good and faithful servant." Conversely, I can think of no greater ruin than to run the race in vain and be disqualified.

Let me ask you a question: Are you willing to commit yourself to finishing the race?

If you are a Christian, I am sure you have heard many and varied challenges to commit your life to Christ. And you have no doubt been asked on several occasions to continue on with Him. I am not, on this occasion, asking either of these. I am calling you to commit yourself, whatever the cost, to finishing the race. To *not* quit. Ever. For the Scriptures are clear that salvation is holistic, and includes *being born again, running well,* and *enduring to the end.* The holy ones of God are called upon to participate in each phase.

When I talk about finishing the race, I do not mean deciding to do so in your own energy, for that would not be attainable. Paul corrected those who tried such a thing when he wrote, "Are you so foolish? Having begun in the Spirit, are you now being made perfect by the flesh?" (Galatians 3:3).

Instead, I am asking you, as one set apart from common use unto God, to commit yourself to finishing that for which you have been called, to do so in faith, relying upon the strength and power of God. For one reason we were granted that strength and power in the first place was to run and win. Listen to the ancient prophet Isaiah, in chapter 40:28–31:

> Has thou not known? has thou not heard, that the everlasting God, the Lord, the Creator of the ends of the earth, fainteth not, neither is weary? there is no searching of his understanding.

> He giveth power to the faint; and to them that have no might he increaseth strength. Even the youths shall faint and be weary, and the young men shall utterly fall:

> But they that wait upon the Lord shall renew their strength; they shall mount up with wings as eagles; they shall run, and not be weary; they shall walk, and not faint.

Do you see who is granted the strength to run and win? *It is those who know they cannot do it on their own!* God promises to "giveth power to the faint." Thus, the holy ones of God throughout history have been earmarked as men and women who did not count their lives dear unto themselves—people of whom the world is not worthy, who set their minds and hearts on crossing the finish line, *no matter what.*

It is when we commit ourselves to walk with Christ to the end that extra strength from Him is supplied. "Being confident of this very thing, that He who has begun a good work in you will complete it until the day of Jesus Christ" (Philippians 1:6).

(*See* Appendix B for Julius Hare's moving sermon on the historical summary of faith in the Church: "The Cloud of Witnesses.")

Part II
Moving Back
Toward Center

6

Beyond "Positional Truth"

By way of review, we have said that holiness means the people of God are set apart from that which is common unto Him. We are transferred from the kingdom of darkness into the Kingdom of His beloved Son. We have noted that God does not make us holy simply as decoration, but to serve Him. Serving Him means being called to action, which in turn calls for power from on high to do His bidding. We have discussed the roadblocks we must overcome to live righteously, as well as the importance of perseverance—of commitment.

We have also referred to God's commands. Under both the Old and New Covenants, holy people have been called upon to live godly lives. Such godly behavior is described in the Ten Commandments. (*See* Appendix A.) But, as we have said, it is not enough to simply know the Law, nor even to agree with it. We are to do it.

Though the Law reveals sin, and tells us what is right, it does not give us the power to live righteous lives. Thus, in this chapter we will consider the power God offers us for personal holiness, for service, and for righteousness. Believe me, it is a power that can change you and me, the Church, and bring salt and light to the world.

THE POWER TO CHANGE THE WORLD

Holiness is not some "extra accessory," added on to the Gospel. It is part and parcel of our salvation, not something separate from it. In other words, salvation itself is designed to set us apart unto God from that which is common. There is no better proof of this fact than to review what God has done for us in the context of Paul's letter to the Romans—sometimes called "the book of full salvation." Let's look at this amazing book in the light of the power for righteousness to impact our surroundings.

71

Our Personal Sin: Romans 1–3a. Any time that we talk about holiness, we must begin by dealing with release from sin. In the first three chapters of his letter, the apostle tells us in no uncertain terms that "all have sinned and fall short of the glory of God" (Romans 3:23). In these early chapters, we see how we have disobeyed the law of God, how we have rejected whatever we have seen of the character of God revealed in creation, and how we have even transgressed our own consciences—that built-in detector of right and wrong.

Thus, all of us stand before God as condemned. Because of the power of sin inherent within us, because of our own willful disobedience to the Lord, we simply do not measure up to His righteousness. As the Scripture says, we are "by nature children of wrath" (Ephesians 2:3). We are utterly common: we need to be cleansed; we need to be made holy.

Made Right With God: Romans 3b–5. Near the end of Romans 3, and throughout chapters 4 and 5, we find the next major theme of Paul's letter and the basic and crucial step toward our salvation: justification by faith. To be justified means to be cleansed from our sins and made righteous in God's sight.

It is my conviction that many Christians who struggle with holiness have either forgotten (or have never been taught) the riches of justification by faith through Jesus Christ. In a sense, justification is "square one" of our relationship to God. Justification is that dynamic flow of God's grace, in which He says to us, "I will take you as you are, even with your sin, and will cleanse you to the point where it is as though you had never sinned in the first place. I will give My very righteousness and purity to you—all free of charge."

Justification is, in a certain sense, a legal matter. We have the Law of God as our standard. Because of sin, we consistently fall short of that Law and thus are declared guilty. The penalty is death. In the death of Jesus Christ, the death penalty is paid for us. Because He died in our place, we are given the benefit of His death, namely, we no longer must die to pay for our sins. The penalty has been paid for us.

And, as though that were not enough, all of Christ's righteousness is given to you as well. Never mind just yet how it comes to apply to you. The point is that "by one Man's righteous act the free gift came to all men, resulting in justification of life" (Romans 5:18).

I have an acquaintance who used to work in a bank. He tells a story of staying after work one night to balance the books. As he was alone in the bank building, going over the various ledgers of the deposits and withdrawals of the day, the thought came to him that God has books to be balanced, too. He told the story this way to a group of us:

> As I was going through the books, my thoughts turned to my own personal ledger. It was as though in my imagination I turned to that record of credits and debits and saw listed under my name the incredibly long list of sins that I had committed during my lifetime. I realized, too, that my deficit balance included not only what I had done, but what I am: a person who, by nature, is disobedient to God.
>
> It was then the Holy Spirit reminded me that, though this condition and list of sins certainly exist and are real, written across that page are the glorious words TRANSFERRED TO THE ACCOUNT OF JESUS CHRIST. I realized anew that night that everything I am and the things I have done which are against the will of God have been paid in my behalf through the blood of God's eternal Son.
>
> Then in my mind, I turned to the account of Jesus Christ, at first expecting to find a listing of not only my own sins but of those of the entire world. Instead, to my most pleasant surprise, I found not the sins (for they had been cancelled), but instead, page upon page of righteousness that alone is His. And then I realized that written across these pages were the words TRANS-FERRED TO THE ACCOUNTS OF ALL WHO BELIEVE.

And so it is that we are justified by faith. Everything that we have ever done, or ever will do, that transgresses God's righteousness has been paid for and taken out of the way through the death of Jesus Christ and because of His blood. Then, credited to our accounts, so to speak, is all of His righteousness, so that we may stand before the Lord without condemnation. We can say with the apostle Paul, "Therefore, having been justified by faith, we have peace with God through our Lord Jesus Christ" (Romans 5:1).

Furthermore, justification reconciles us to God—that is, it reestablishes a broken fellowship with Him—cancelling out the debt of our sin that stood between us and Him. As Paul writes in Romans 5:10, "For if when we were enemies we were reconciled to God by the death of His Son, much more, having been reconciled, we shall be saved by His life." Thus, like Abraham, we can be called the friends of God.

How does this apply to personal holiness? "For both He who sanctifies and those who are being sanctified are all of one, for which reason He is not ashamed to call them brethren" (Hebrews 2:11). We who are justified are likewise set apart (or sanctified) by Jesus Christ to the Father. Set apart unto God, we are one family, together with our Lord Jesus Christ; He calls us brothers and sisters. We are family and we are friends. This does not mean, by the way, that we view Him as a cosmic buddy or as a common sibling. Instead, we see Him as the Lord God Almighty who, through the will of His Father, has condescended to take upon Himself our own humanity and be identified with us, and change us into the image of His glorified human nature.

There is something else to be said concerning justification. Although we speak of being justified by faith, we must take care to underscore that it is not *our* faith that justifies us. Rather, it is God in His mercy who justifies. His justification is received by faith, but as with any gift from God, it is offered through His mercy and grace, and is merited by nothing—not even our faith.

To put it another way, justification is based on what God does, not on what we do. The beloved old Bible student Herbert Lockyer writes in *Victory:* "We readily admit that there are a good many moral, religious people who are like Christ in their actions, but such actions are simply the product of the natural man. Holiness, however, can never be reproduced: it is a gift of God. The greatest enemy of holiness is morality. One can be moral without being holy, but never holy without being moral."

We do not even gain standing with God by perfect Christian living. He declares us righteous, no matter how much we have sinned. It is God's mercy which gives us constant confidence before Him and in our relationship with Him—not what we might think we bring to Him.

Crucial for us to understand is that justification is active and dynamic. It is not static, just as God's other gifts, such as love and joy, peace and redemption are not static. It is the past, present, and future ongoing action of God which credits Christ's righteousness to you *this very moment.* And on that basis, justification continues to motivate us to love and good works. And while these good works do not increase our justification, the doing of them increases our faith.

In marriage, a husband and wife are placed in right relationship with each other. On a human level, this right standing could be said to parallel justification. At our house, Marilyn attends Saint Athanasius Academy four mornings a week, auditing Bible and theology classes. I work in my office at home. On days when I'm not hopelessly overloaded, I'll take a morning break to do a good work—cleaning up the kitchen (with a rake!) after our six children have had breakfast there. That's my "surprise" to her when she comes home at noon.

Doing this for her in no way gets us more married. But there's no question that such surprises serve to deepen our love. Things like this help keep a relationship alive and growing. It is in this way that our justification, our right relationship with God is dynamic, causing us to serve Him by doing things which show Him our love. Good works do not make us "more justified," but they do deepen our capacity to grow in faith and love for Christ.

Having said all of this, then, it is important to our Christian growth that we do not isolate justification by faith as a doctrine apart from all the other gifts God gives to us. For justification by itself will not produce righteous behavior—which is why Romans does not end with chapter 5. On the other hand, you must have this matter of justification and right standing with God fixed in your heart, or you will never consistently walk in holiness. Those whose hearts condemn them before God struggle futilely for a life and conduct set apart to God. But the grace of God *received* and *accepted* in justification frees our hearts from condemnation in order to pursue holiness as we walk in the Spirit.

A Living Union: Romans 6. In the same action by which we are justified before God by faith, we are brought into a living union with Jesus Christ (Romans, chapter 6). It is God the Holy Spirit who effects this union, a union by which we receive the power to live a godly life. This means that we are brought into union with Jesus Christ in and through His glorified human nature.

At this point, it is vital for us to understand something of the Incarnation of our Lord Jesus Christ. In Him complete divinity is brought into union with complete humanity—without confusion, without change, without division, without separation—as the Creed of Chalcedon declares. In baptism, believers are united to Christ in His death, burial, and Resurrection. Thus, we are joined to Christ through His humanity, and by that union our Savior, our Mediator, brings us into relationship with God the Father.

And how is such a union with Christ effected? Let us allow Romans 6:3–8 to speak for itself:

> Or do you not know that as many of us as were baptized into Christ Jesus were baptized into His death? Therefore we were buried with Him by baptism into death, that just as Christ was raised from the dead by the glory of the Father, even so we also should walk in newness of life. For if we have been united together in the likeness of His death, certainly we also shall be in the likeness of His resurrection, knowing this, that our old man was crucified with Him, that the body of sin might be done away with, that we should no longer serve sin. For he who has died has been freed from sin. Now if we died with Christ, we believe that we shall also live with Him.

As Paul so lucidly states, it is through baptism that the faithful are justified, according to God's mercy, and are brought into living union with His Son.

Apart from justification by faith, union with Christ is impossible. And apart from union with Christ, holiness is impossible. It is in Christ that we are set apart unto God. Further, it is Christ who, being holy by nature, has lived out a godly and righteous life. And because His divine nature interpenetrates His human nature, *power is there for us* who are joined to Him. Thus, Christ's righteousness is not only His, but ours as well, who are united with Him.

As bone of His bone, and flesh of His flesh, you are empowered by Him to live in a righteous fashion. You are saved from your fallen estate and from the corruption that is in this world, and are brought—by the water and the Spirit—into union with His glorified humanity. Thus, the apostle Peter so boldly writes, "Baptism now saves us" (*see* 1 Peter 3:21). God the Father has chosen His Holy Spirit to use water baptism as the means or the vehicle through which that union with our Lord Jesus Christ is effected.[4]

The Christian is holy because he is joined to the One whose humanity is united with and interpenetrated by the very divine nature of God Himself. Thus, we who are in Christ are set apart to God, withdrawn from profane or secular use, and are God's special property.

And before we move from Holy Baptism into Romans 7, let me say something about another crucial sacrament. We have in our day dangerously ignored the role of Holy Communion in securing us in holy living. To ignore communion, to pass it by, or to receive it when willful sin prevails in our lives, promotes weakness and illness. And undernourished Christians walk very feebly in the grace of God. In large part, I believe this is what separates the sort of lives we live in the twentieth century from the lives of Christians who were faithful to God in the early Church. (For further reading along these lines, I suggest my earlier book *The Physical Side of Being Spiritual* [Zondervan].)

In the Protestant tradition, many Christians have an understanding of union with Christ merely as *idea* or concept. Thus, many find great frustration in trying to apply union with Christ to daily living. Such modern man-made categories as "positional versus experiential" or "state and standing" pop up all the time in our religious vocabularies, when we try to explain what our union with Jesus Christ is all about. We end up "spiritualizing" the Bible, instead of taking what God says at face value. Such frustration will continue as long as (1) we do not see our union with Christ as one of substance; and, (2) as long as that union is disconnected from the sacraments. We must again become *doers* of the Word of God, not just hearers.[5]

Jesus said:

> Most assuredly, I say to you, unless you eat the flesh of the Son of Man and drink His blood, you have no life in you. Whoever eats My flesh and drinks My blood has eternal life, and I will raise him up at the last day.

> For My flesh is food indeed, and My blood is drink indeed. He who eats My flesh and drinks My blood dwells in Me, and I in him.   John 6:53–56

Cyril of Alexandria, in his commentary on this passage, imagines someone who is reluctant to partake in the Holy Supper saying, "I am refusing to partake because it is written, 'Whoever eats the bread and drinks the cup of the Lord in an unworthy manner, eats and drinks judgment to himself.' I have examined myself and see that I am not worthy."

"But," asks Cyril of that man, "when will you be worthy? For if you are always going to be scared away from the Table by your stumblings, you will never stop stumbling. Do this: Decide to lead a holier life, in harmony with the Law, and go ahead and receive the Blessing of the Table—believing that it has not only the power over spiritual death but all our spiritual diseases as well. For by it, Christ in us silences the law which rages in the members of our flesh, kindles piety toward God, and deadens our passions. Not imputing our transgressions to us, He heals us."[6]

There is nothing so disheartening as visiting a Church and finding the people either avoiding the special communion services (as so often happens in Protestant churches) or passing up the opportunity to partake of the holy elements (as happens in some Episcopal, Orthodox, and Roman Catholic churches). No wonder so many of our churches are dead, and so many of our people living ungodly lives! Let us embrace the Holy Table in love and faith. It is the people who are united there, where Christ told us to be, who are in the best position in the universe to change the world!

A New Commandment: Romans 7. In Romans 7, we find that we, who are justified by faith and are in union with Christ, are brought out from under obedience to the law through human effort, and now obey commands of the Holy Spirit, which are written on our hearts and minds through newness of life. Thus, we are led by the Spirit and not by a static set of ordinances. For "We have been delivered from the law, having died to what we were held by, so that we should serve in the newness of the Spirit and not in the oldness of the letter" (Romans 7:6).

The stabilizing factor here is that the Law has not changed. As Paul also writes in Romans 7:12, "The law is holy, and the commandment [is] holy and just and good." We must never be antinomian or "anti-Law." The Law of God endures forever; it does not change. Instead it is *we* who have been changed. It is *we* who have been justified, brought into vital union with Christ, and whose hearts have been made soft through the Holy Spirit.

The Life-giving Spirit: Romans 8. In Romans 8, Paul presents to us the One who ensures that our justification, our union with Christ, our sensitivity to God's will, remain active and alive. Of course, I'm talking about the third Person of the Trinity, the Holy Spirit. God the Holy Spirit keeps on releasing us from our fallen human state and constantly activates us in our standing and union with Jesus Christ. Several things come into play here.

- He releases us from the condemnation of sin and death.
- He accomplishes something that the Law could never do: He fulfills its requirements for those of us who walk in His power.
- He promises life to our mortal bodies.
- He helps us put to death the deeds of unrighteousness.
- As we respond to His leading, He validates that we are God's children.
- He helps us when we are weak.
- He intercedes for us.
- He causes all things to work together for good according to God's purpose.
- He seals God's promise of hope within our hearts.

The story is told of the housewife who was startled one day to see a mouse scampering across the pantry floor. She immediately went to the basement to find a mousetrap to catch the unwelcome guest. With the trap in hand, she opened the refrigerator, looking in vain for some cheese. There was none to be had.

Earlier that day she had read through *Better Homes and Gardens,* and had recalled seeing some delicious looking Swiss cheese pictured in a four-color ad. *Maybe I can substitute the picture for the real thing,* she thought. She found a scissors, retrieved the magazine, and carefully cut off a corner of the cheese. Gingerly she glued the picture of the cheese on the latch of the trap, set the spring, and placed the apparatus on the pantry floor near the baseboard.

The next morning she was shocked and dismayed as she looked into the pantry. The trap had snapped all right. But all she caught was a picture of a mouse!

Hebrews says the Law is a shadow (or picture) of the good things to come and not the very form of things (Hebrews 10:1). It is a *real* picture of *real* righteousness to be sure. But it can never *make* us righteous. Only God can, through His forgiveness, His justification, our union with Christ, and the power of His Holy Spirit. This is why we never *stop* with simply "getting the picture" of what is right and wrong. For that will only bring us the pictures or concepts of righteousness. We do not stop with what some call "positional righteousness." Instead, we move on into the vital reality of obeying the life-giving Holy Spirit who lives within us.

In short, the Holy Spirit enables the holy ones of God to live righteous lives in this present age. He is constantly there as our prompter and encourager; He will not let us alone! We read nothing here of the Holy Spirit making us passive, doing everything through us. No, we are *actively* obedient, *actually* righteous. As we listen to Him, He is constantly revealing the Word of God to us in the Church.

Holy Ones on Display: Romans 9–11. In Romans 9, 10, and 11, one of the glorious—but often forgotten—purposes of the Church is revealed. We as the people of God are to be a continual "show-and-tell-time" to the Old Covenant nation, Israel, which has rejected Jesus Christ as Messiah. The holiness, which was promised to Israel, has now been made available to all who believe.

In this present age, Israel, by and large, has rejected the Lord, even as the apostle John wrote long ago: "He came to His own, and His own did not receive Him. But as many as received Him, to them He gave the right to become children of God, even to those who believe in His name" (John 1:11, 12).

Paul now turns his attention to these, his kinsmen, and shows how this new holy nation, the Church, the new Israel, is now the display case for what God promsies to all who are justified and brought into union with His anointed One. Israel could have had these riches, but turned them down. This truth is magnified in Romans, chapter 10, verses 19–21, when Paul writes concerning Israel and the Church:

> But I say, did Israel not know? First Moses says:
> "I will provoke you to jealousy by those
> who are not a nation, And by a foolish
> nation I will anger you."
>
> But Isaiah is very bold and says:
> "I was found by those who did not
> seek Me; I was made manifest to
> those who did not ask for Me."
>
> But to Israel he says:
> "All day long I have stretched
> out My hands To a disobedient
> and contrary people."

Here we catch a glimpse of what Paul is going to expand upon in the last five chapters of his letter: Holy living is not accomplished through individualism, nor do we bear witness to Israel merely on a one-on-one basis. It takes a whole nation to make another nation jealous. And until modern Christians are willing to see themselves as a *nation,* and bring their lives into relationship with Christ *in His Church,* hope for personal holiness in the fullest sense of the word will be thwarted.

People, holiness cannot be developed any other way! In fact, it is embarrassing to see many who have loved the Scriptures and who have preached with so fervent a zeal for Christ, displaying such unholy behavior. Instead of ministering to the poor, you have people asking the poor to send $5 or $10 a month for $50-million-plus-a-year television programs. Instead of building godly congregations, religious entrepreneurs, operating outside the Church, have grouped around themselves clienteles of followers sponsoring visionary programs and strategies utterly foreign to the Holy Scriptures.

Patently, such behavior will never make Israel jealous. What is the answer?

The Name of the Game Is Church: Romans 12-16. Starting in Romans, chapter 12, and continuing on through chapter 16, the apostle Paul urges us all to "present your bodies a living sacrifice, holy, acceptable to God, which is your reasonable service" (v. 1). In short, he calls us to be *Church.*

In Romans 12, we are told how holy people get along with one another, how the gifts of the Holy Spirit operate in the Church, and how to respond to one another in various circumstances. In chapter 13, we are told how holy people behave under civil government. We are challenged to obey governmental authorities, and to pay our taxes to support them. In chapter 14, we are told how holy people respond in situations that are not always black and white. Because in Christ we have been set free, we operate according to His love. In chapter 15, we are instructed to live godly lives, preferring our brothers and sisters in Christ before ourselves. We bear each other's burdens as we worship the Lord together. And in chapter 16, Paul's own love for the people of God is underscored as he gives his personal greetings to them all. Notice how he knew the people under his charge by name!

It seems almost to be a sign of the times that we modern Christians constantly emphasize Romans 1-8, which is in itself glorious, at the expense of Romans 9-16, which speaks of how holiness operates corporately in Christ. Take either section, and you have only half the story. Take them both together—where you have powerful personal holiness in the first half and powerful corporate behavior in the second half—and you have a force the gates of hell can never reckon with.

All of this is to say that there is no one, final, isolated "secret" to holiness. You do not become holy just through understanding justification. You do not become holy only through union with Christ, nor do you become holy through freedom from the Law; nor through the fullness of the Spirit alone; nor even by proper functioning in the Church.

Beloved, it is *all* these things that secure your ongoing righteousness! In "the gospel according to Romans" it is those who repent from their sin (1–3) who are justified by faith (4–5), who come into union with Christ (6), who are released from the Law (7), and controlled by the Holy Spirit (8), who are membered in the Church (9–11), and whose lives are on the line day and night in the Body of Christ (12–16) who are the holy ones of God.

Isn't this the faith of the Fathers, the scholastics, the Reformers? We do not "snapshot" the Scriptures, living out an isolated doctrine or emphasis here and there, and expect to come up holy and godly. Holiness, rather, is the total ministry of Jesus Christ to us, ranging all the way from our individual hearts to the indestructible Church.

God forbid us from *ever* settling for anything less.

THE JOYFUL CONSEQUENCES OF HOLINESS

Who can fully name the infinite fruit and glory that comes in the Church when its people live holy and godly lives? Let's conclude this section by singling out just three consequences of godly living.

First of all, *God Himself is truly honored.* Holiness, above all else, is to the Lord. God is holy, and He desires that we be holy by participation in His holiness. Heaven is honored when on earth His people are righteous in their conduct. The apostle Peter writes, "But as He who has called you is holy, you also be holy in all your conduct, because it is written, 'Be holy, for I am holy.' " (1 Peter 1:15, 16). We are a people set apart unto God, called to glorify Him in all of our actions.

A second consequence of holiness is that *our fellow inhabitors of this earth learn of the holiness of God when they see it lived out in the lives of His saints.* After all, it is only reasonable that those who participate in a relationship with God through union with Jesus Christ in His Church should be like the Lord whom they serve. This is how the Church of God ministers the holiness of God to a world in great need of seeing it. As we have seen, part of the purpose of the Church is to send forth from its ranks the very righteousness of Christ Himself, as it is disseminated through the lives of His people.

A third consequence of personal holiness is *our own assurance of faith.* Think back to times when you have obeyed the Lord and done His will in the face of great cost. Remember experiencing the sense of His presence and pleasure in a special way? Many Christians struggle with the assurance of salvation, because they know they lack personal holiness. They question their devotion to God, and the reality of their worship fades. This is no surprise, is it? For one who serves a holy God, who has been saved through the life-giving flesh of Jesus Christ, and has been granted a measure of the Holy Spirit, fully expects that there should be a strong measure of personal righteousness coming forth from his life.

Therefore, the Scriptures teach, and we must conclude, that personal holiness is no option for the Christian. *It is a necessary part of the life we have in Jesus Christ.* Without it, we will not see the Lord. All that is necessary for our righteousness has been made available by God Himself. We are left lacking in no way. We simply need to walk, in obedience of faith, in what He has told us to do and to be.

7

A Forgotten Friend

It has always seemed to me that the late 1960s was a most unusual time for us in this country to receive and love the smash Broadway hit, and later, the film *Fiddler on the Roof*. Here we were, in the midst of those highly antiestablishment and turbulent years socially, morally, and politically. And all of a sudden, along comes Tevya, bounding enthusiastically across the stage singing, "Tra—*di*—tion!" I can still hear the music; I savored every moment of it.

Somehow, even though "doing your own thing" was the order of the day, people wanted to crawl out of their theater seats onto the stage and join that dramatic family! A general public, which allegedly hated tradition, ended up loving this and wanting more.

I predict that in the 1980s and 90s, there will be a significant swing by the evangelical public back toward Church tradition and continuity with our past. Coming off the days of hapless liberalism in the churches in the 1930s, many Christians, perhaps with some reason, seemed to want to break out of the traces of whatever was left in traditional Christianity, and to ask God to "do something new." But there's a potentially dangerous mentality about always wanting new experiences or emphases. The pitfall is that it becomes very easy to leave the old foundations, and unwittingly build on new, not necessarily stronger ones.

At a time when Israel had gone dry spiritually, a promise of the Lord came to the prophet Isaiah, "And they that shall be of thee shall build the old waste places: thou shalt raise up the foundations of many generations; and thou shalt be called, The repairer of the breach, The restorer of paths to dwell in" (Isaiah 58:12). The psalmist David said, "If the foundations be destroyed, what can the righteous do?" (Psalms 11:3). Note, it's the *old* foundations that are restored. And I sense that more and more evangelical and charismatic Christians are seeing the need for a return to orthodoxy and historicity in their faith and worship. We have grown lonely, haven't we, for true Christian tradition?

THE BIBLE ON TRADITION

Did you know that being traditional is part of being holy—and of being salt and light to the world—as long as it's the right kind of tradition? In fact, throughout the long history of the Christian Church, there has been something called *holy* tradition. The Bible tells us so.

First off, the Scriptures in no uncertain terms warn us against what is called "the tradition of men." To follow that tradition is unholy, because it is fabricated by unholy men.

One of the most scathing indictments Jesus ever leveled was that which He hurled against the tradition of those unholy men, the Pharisees and the scribes. Look at His blistering words in Mark 7:5–13.

Then the Pharisees and scribes asked Him, "Why do Your disciples not walk according to the tradition of the elders, but eat bread with unwashed hands?"

He answered and said to them, "Well did Isaiah prophesy of you hypocrites, as it is written: 'This people honors Me with their lips, But their heart is far from Me.

"And in vain they worship Me, Teaching as doctrines the commandments of men.' For laying aside the commandment of God, you hold the tradition of men—the washing of pitchers and cups, and many other such things you do."

And He said to them, "All too well you reject the commandment of God, that you may keep your tradition. For Moses said, 'Honor your father and your mother'; and, 'He who curses father or mother, let him be put to death.' But you say, 'If a man says to his father or mother: Whatever you might be profited by me is Corban (that is, a gift), he shall be free'; and you no longer let him do anything for his father or his mother, making the word of God of no effect through your tradition which you have handed down. And many such things you do."

Here was a case in which unholy tradition stood squarely in the way of an effective ministry of the Word of God: it made null and void what God told His people to do. This is why Paul, in an equally familiar passage, issues the same basic warning Jesus gave: "Beware lest anyone take you captive through philosophy and empty deceit, according to the *tradition* of men, according to the basic principles of the world, and not according to Christ" (Colossians 2:8, italics mine).

Since he manifested such disdain for unholy tradition, Paul's exhortations concerning another kind of tradition given in his second letter to the Thessalonians take on added weight for us: "Therefore, brethren, stand fast and hold the *traditions* which you have been taught, whether by word or our epistle" (2:15, italics mine). And, "Now we command you, brethren, in the name of our Lord Jesus Christ, that you withdraw from every brother who walks disorderly and not according to the *tradition* which he received from us" (3:6, italics mine).

After having warned Christians not to follow tradition, here Paul tells them to "stand firm" in it—and to avoid those who do not! What is the difference? Simply this: The warnings are against the unholy traditions of men, the exhortations are to follow the holy traditions of *God,* given by Him to the Church through the holy Apostles. We will never change the world, apart from bringing ourselves back to these age-old foundations.

SOMETHING OLD, SOMETHING NEW

Before we talk about how holy traditions help us toward our pursuit of holiness, that by it we might change the world, and how we can distinguish good tradition from bad, we had better first deal with another issue. That is, can God give us traditions which cannot be found in the Scriptures?

For instance, what about Sunday school? Is it a tradition of God or of men? If it is a tradition of men, then how has it gotten into virtually all our churches? Could it be that God has given us a new tradition, one that, while never commanded directly in the Scriptures, certainly has been accepted by the Church? What of the altar call, the Wednesday-evening service, the alb and stole, the sign of the cross, church choirs, annotated Bibles? Does the Church have from its Head, Jesus Christ, the authority to instigate such practices? How do we know? And what are the safeguards?

Honestly, I ask these things, as one who in the past has been horribly roughshod in decrying tradition. Having been brought up in a Church quite heavy in tradition, and then coming to a vital personal faith in Christ as a young adult, I was convinced that things like tradition, liturgy, and form produced spiritual death by the

loads. But, after nearly two decades of what I prized as
taneous, Spirit-led Christianity," I discovered, to my chagrin,
our crowd of nontraditional people was fast developing tradi-
s all our own—so much our own, in fact, that I was forced into
specting that they might even be the traditions of men.

In my years of searching for the meaning of the Church, a group
of us, largely from evangelical and charismatic backgrounds,
courageously decided to meet together on Sunday mornings for a
free-flowing worship (as we called it). These were people who had
been highly critical of the organized church. One of our brethren
used to say, "The trouble with my old church was that nothing new
ever happened. You could look at what was going on in our order of
worship and know within five minutes what time it was! Let's see—
the Lord's Prayer—that means it's 11:20."

So we decided to meet without any special order of worship.
(What we almost had was *dis*order.) But scarcely six months had
passed, before it became obvious that pattern and form had begun
to develop once again. We met in a living room to get away fro
the idea of rows and rows of pews. It occurred to me one morni
as we met, that the same people always sat in the same chairs.
embarrassing was my realization that the same brother pray
opening prayer at least 90 percent of the time each Sunday
was essentially the same "spontaneous" prayer each week
something like this:

> Thank You, Lord, that we are able to meet here in
> and in truth, not being controlled by men but simp
> by Your Spirit. Thank You for the freedom of such
> pray that You will lead, guide, and direct us int
> God might get the glory. In Jesus' name. *Ame*

(*By the way,* the fact that I had unconsci
prayer, because of its weekly repetition,
about how set prayers emerged in the an
never a meeting behind closed doors to d
these prayers would be. Rather, as the
Church from week to week, that whic
prayers" became a normal part of t'

Within six months I became e
when I discovered you could ess

ship services, too. And the only real diffe...
First Baptist or First Presbyterian was the ...
more casual dress—and the fact we insiste...
whereas, they admitted they did.

Let me encourage you with a very important bit...
dition is not your enemy. It never has been, and never ...
liturgy and form your foe. Your enemy is sin and death. ...
lief. And the devil.

It's like the child who is brought up to memorize and lo...
Scriptures. And then he rebels. Is that the fault of Holy Script...
God forbid! No, it sounds more like the devil has been at work...
perhaps through legalism. May we be delivered from making the ...
Bible, or holy tradition, or the Church the problem. Such allega-
tions come very close to ascribing to Satan the works of God.

THE ESSENTIALS OF HOLY TRADITION

In his book *Orthodoxy,* C. K. Chesterton speaks directly and
plainly to the issue of tradition when he writes, "Tradition means
giving votes to the most obscure of all classes, our ancestors." Even
the person who holds to a basically congregational stance in Church
polity should at least give the "one-man/one-vote" privilege to
those of the past.

There was a man who lived in the fifth century who was to the
Church of his day much the same as someone like the late C. S.
Lewis would be to our day. Vincent of Lerins gave us his "Three
Ways to Tell If Something Traditional Is From God or Not." Vin-
cent gives us this helpful threefold checklist for evaluating what
makes for trustworthy tradition:

1. *Universality*—being sure that an interpretation of Scripture
   or a practice is held to by the *entire Church* all over the world.

2. *Antiquity*—not deviating from those interpretations held as
   far back as possible in Christian ancestry.

3. *Consensus*—once antiquity is established, adopting the *common* interpretations of all, or almost all, the Christian bishops
   and scholars.

With this sort of handle on tradition—and this is the way tradition historically have been weighed in the Church—our basis for
accepting tradition, as it is held up to the scrutiny of Holy Scrip-

ture, is gloriously stabilized. None of these three components in and of itself is adequate, but using them in concert with one another gives a great measure of surety. Writing prior to A.D 450, Saint Vincent goes on to lambast those he calls "modernists," and he warns his readers never to trust "the sacreligious rashness of a single man to the Church of Christ."[7]

MAKING TRADITION WORK FOR YOU

You might be saying, "Fine, but I don't get the point of all this. How does knowing and living in Christian tradition help in my everyday life? How does tradition promote outreach for Christ?"

Let's take as an example the generally unpleasant experience of having cultists—such as Mormons or Jehovah's Witnesses—come to your door. Perhaps on occasion they have eased their way inside. Politely, you let them state their case.

Then, you may say, "How about hearing my side of the story?" You reach for your Bible and start in.

To your frustration and dismay, they come right back at you with an equal number of Bible verses of their own. So you give them some more. And they give *you* some more—a few of which you had never thought about before. It is at this point they often begin to attract a new convert. For if it is *just* your Scripture verses against theirs, even if you do not bend to their doctrine, you will sense you have come away from the argument the loser.

This is why Wheaton College professor Robert Webber makes such a pointed statement to people who, because of their zeal to insist Scripture is true, sometimes overlook the need to be sure their *opinions* on the biblical message are correct. He writes in *Common Roots,* "Evangelicals should come to grips with the fact that the Bible belongs to the Church. It is the living Church that receives, guards, passes on, and interprets Scripture. Consequently, the modern individualistic approach to interpretation of Scripture should give way to the authority of what the Church has always believed, taught, and passed down in history."

It is the *Church,* which through its history has received and disseminated the biblical message, that determines orthodox theology. To hold otherwise is to say, "I alone will decide what Scripture means." And authority becomes individualistic: each man before God with his open Bible—or as the apostle Peter calls it "private interpretation" (2 Peter 1:20).

I will never forget the day that God used me as His instrument to bring my first Jehovah's Witness to faith in Jesus Christ. If you are anything like me, you do not like to lose. And I had lost battle after battle with these people over the years, as they came to my door. It always ended up with my set of Bible verses against theirs. But in showing her the Scripture in light of the common faith of the Church—the orthodox faith, if you will—it was a whole new ball game.

We went head to head, doctrine to doctrine. It was now no longer me and my Bible against her and her Bible. Instead, it was what her source, Charles Russell, said about the Scriptures versus holy tradition on the teaching of the Scriptures: those truths held by the Church Councils, the early Fathers of the Church, the later Fathers, the Reformers, the Wesleyan leaders, the Puritans, and contemporary Christian teachers. Over and over again, I was able to hammer home, "You mean you will stake your eternal destiny on the doctrinal guesswork of Mr. Charles Taze Russell, when *the entire believing Church* says, 'No, it's not that way'?"

And on we went into the biblical passages on eternal punishment, those on the eternally begotten Son of the Father, the Three Persons of the Godhead, who fully share One Divine Nature, and the rest. We went into John 1 on the Word becoming flesh and into Hebrews 1 where God the Father addresses God the Son as "Lord." Not just my interpretation against hers, but the witness of the entire mainstream Church of our Lord Jesus Christ through history against the aberrant allegations of heretic Charles Russell.

Finally, praise be to God, our side won! She confessed the Lord Jesus Christ and turned her life over to Him. Believe me, it was a team effort. For the Holy Spirit worked sovereignly on her heart, not through one man alone, but through scores and scores of His servants from the past. Together we whipped the forces of darkness.

WE ARE FAMILY!

Sometimes people assume that when you say that Church tradition determines what is orthodox doctrine, you have slipped into the rut of making the Church Fathers' or the Reformers' authority equal to or greater than that of the Scriptures. No! It's absolutely the opposite. It is because these men of God subjected themselves to the inspiration and authority of the Scriptures that we listen to them so attentively.

Furthermore, when we say we listen to the historic voices of the leaders of the Church, we do not mean we believe every statement each one of these historic leaders makes. Of course not. What we look for is consensus. What do they all teach that is a common interpretation of Scripture? That is what we are after.

And these understandings of Scripture on major doctrinal issues have been ratified by councils, churches, denominations, and so forth, down to the present day. This is why the great Creeds of the Church are so vital. For these Creeds (such as the Apostles' Creed, the Nicene Creed, and the Chalcedonian Creed) were the outgrowth of the battles of the Early Church against heresies. Thus, for example, when the blasphemer Arius came along in the early fourth century, claiming there was a time when the Son of God did not exist, and that the Son was not fully equal with the Father, the leaders of the Church came together to speak with one voice what the Apostles taught concerning these matters. And out of that debate at Nicaea in A.D. 325 came the richest statement of the true biblical doctrine on the Person of our Lord Jesus Christ the Church has ever known: the Nicene Creed.

While we do not substitute the Nicene Creed for Scripture (only the Scriptures are God-breathed), neither do we substitute our personal interpretation of Scripture for the Nicene Creed! We *do* subject our interpretations of the Scriptures concerning the Person of Christ to the truths of the Creed *because it sets forth the truths of Scripture.* To do otherwise would be to arrogantly say, "I alone am better able to set forth doctrine concerning the eternal Son of God than is the Church of the living God." This is why, century after century, the Church has earnestly and consistently confessed the truth of the Nicene Creed.

TRADITION AND MORALITY

Just today the phone rang with the news that yet another Bible-believing Christian hired a moving truck, packed up the furniture, and headed for another city, leaving his wife and children behind. What do you say to him, when he not only knows all the Scriptures on the subject of fidelity, but has *memorized* many of them?

Or what do you tell an eighteen-year-old Christian girl who has admitted sleeping with her boyfriend, finds she's pregnant, and now wants an abortion? Or how do you handle the situation of the college man who has "discovered" that he's homosexual, has explained away the Scripture on the subject with an apologetic taught to him by some "Christian homosexual proponent," and now takes up living with his male lover?

By all means, do not neglect the use of the Holy Scriptures in such instances, along with a deep reliance upon the Holy Spirit to give you the right words to say. But remember—you have yet another witness to call in as well when his help is needed: Mr. Tradition.

The tradition of the Church simply does not allow for the contemporary practice of divorce on demand. Anciently, if a marriage partner simply up and decided to head for the door, refusing to obey the vows of holy matrimony exchanged before the Lord, careful discipline by the Church (and often excommunication) was sure to follow. For had not Paul written concerning immorality, "Purge out the old leaven . . ."? (1 Corinthians 5:7). This was not done for punishment, for vengeance is God's alone, but rather to bring about repentance, that the offender might be saved and restored.

As for fornication and perversion, well, John Chrysostom had a word for it: "Truly immorality is a terrible thing, and one that brings everlasting punishment. . . . Wherefore, I beseech, hasten to rid yourself of this disease. Moreover, if you do not obey my words, do not set foot within these sacred portals. I say this for it is not fitting that the sheep that are covered with mange and full of disease mingle with the healthy ones, but they should remain apart from the flock until they are free from the disease."[8]

What if the evangelical Church got tough like this once again, stepping in to care for its faltering marriages and immoral members, having the courage to render godly discipline to those who refused to follow counsel?

Sometime back, a group of Christian ministers from several denominations and churches in the Midwest were meeting together for a time of worship and fellowship. During the two days spent together, one of the men, pastor of a large denominational church, asked for wisdom in dealing with a problem which had arisen in his congregation.

"One of the strongest leaders in my church, the teacher of the one-hundred-and-fifty-member adult Sunday-school class, has been seeing another woman, who is also a member," he said. "I have talked with him about this on two occasions, and he has promised to cut off the affair. But so far, he has not done it. I feel my hands are tied, because he has brought many of the people in that class to Christ. They are in the Church because of him. If I pull him out as the teacher, he may leave and take all those people along with him. What can I do?"

To the man, we told him that biblically—and traditionally—he had no choice. "To maintain holiness in the Church, the man has to be removed from teaching until he truly repents," we explained. "And if no repentance comes about, he should be excommunicated." The pastor was studiously silent.

"Either way, you could lose," we went on. "If the man stays, he will ultimately poison the whole class, maybe the Church. If he is removed and will not repent, he could take fifty people with him. But the issue is not political, it's moral. You need to remove him."

With fear and trembling, this young pastor returned home to render the discipline. The offending teacher was removed from his ministry for a minimum of six months. Great care was given to restore him and his wife, and to give appropriate direction to the other woman involved. To my knowledge, not one person left the class.

Over a year later, I paid the pastor a visit. When I inquired about the adultery situation, I was told with a smile, "He's back!"

Later that day I had an opportunity to meet the wife of the offender. With tears in her eyes, she gave praise and thanks to the Lord for healing the marriage, and for a pastor who had the fortitude to deal in a holy manner with an errant member. That night, tears came to my own eyes as this couple came together to receive Holy Communion.

Discipline is *always* a risk. It must be administered both firmly and tenderly. But whether we are fathers in the home or in the Church, we do not back off from confrontation because of fear. Because sin has crept back into the camp so gradually, many pastors have become like the frog in the biology-class experiment, who perishes without resistance in boiling water, because it is heated up so slowly from a comfortable lukewarm temperature.

And, as with adultery and divorce, so the historic Church has consistently stood against abortion as an alternative to an unwanted pregnancy. In doing so, it would offer great care for an unwed mother and the newborn child, working fervently to bring repentance, healing, and holiness back into the situation. And throughout its history, the Church has interpreted the Holy Scriptures to mean exactly what they say about homosexuality: It is sin, and those who persist in it will, like other persistent sinners, not enter the Kingdom of God.

What added strength in Christian preaching and personal guidance to say to an offender: "Look, it's not your word against mine, or your interpretation of the Bible against mine. This is where the Church of our Lord Jesus Christ, including the Apostles, the Fathers, the Doctors, the Reformers, the Puritans, and today's Christians have stood. I beg you, do not oppose His entire Church in heaven and on earth, and bet your whims against God's righteous judgment."

TRADITION AND GODLINESS

Every sincere Christian is to be about the business of godliness. We want to have and to know that sort of godliness, which will equip us to see the Lord on the last day. If we choose to circumvent holy tradition, the attainment of such godliness will be impossible. Such a choice would mean we aim to define and claim God's righteousness on our own, apart from the holy and faithful who have preceded us in the Church.

As a matter of fact, to deny the tradition of God is to hold to and obey the tradition of men. For it is *men's traditions* which tell us that we should all believe the Bible as we choose, and not pay attention to the godly ones of the past. This is not to negate the teaching of the Holy Spirit to the individual believer. It is wise to note, however, that humanistic and godless tradition can produce rebellion and hatred for authority and disdain for the Church. It is a *modernism* which teaches that only what we believe today is relevant. Holy tradition urges us to listen to the saints who have gone on before, to hold to their faith, their doctrine, their sense of morality and commitment to the Holy Scriptures. And by the way, great biographies of such people—all the way from Foxe's *Book of Martyrs* to Elisabeth Elliot's *Shadow of the Almighty*—make for great reading.

And there is one more thing that holy tradition will help you see: the *apostasy* of the past. For to be traditional in no way means you automatically accept everything in the past, just because it happens to be old. Rather, holy tradition calls us to bow to the *truth* of universal witness, antiquity, and consensus of holy brothers and sisters in Christ who, throughout history, have fervently followed and obeyed Him, in many cases to the death. It was such a love for the traditional faith that prompted the song:

> Faith of our fathers, living still
> In spite of dungeon, fire and sword—
> O how our hearts beat high with joy
> Whene'er we hear that glorious word:
> Faith of our fathers, holy faith,
> We will be true to thee till death!

The choice is ours: we can stand with them, or we can stand apart from them. But if we reject the holy traditions they preserved and kept for us, then we are bringing an immense charge against God's elect, and placing ourselves as judges over all. Further, we will never change the world. Saint of God, do not let what they fought for be forgotten. Take holy tradition as your friend.

8

The Zone of Safety

It was a sobering conversation.

I was visiting with a young pastor on the staff of one of the huge and influential evangelical churches in this country, and we talked on into the evening of our vision for Christendom. His commitment to Christ and the Church seemed unwaving and set for life.

As we discussed where things had come from in American Christianity over the past couple of decades, and where the Church seemed to be heading in the next ten or twenty years, the conversation turned to the looming number of other seemingly dedicated Christians—some of the most highly gifted Bible teachers, preachers, and leaders—who for reasons of unholiness and apostasy were no longer aboard ship.

"What is it that gets them off track?" he asked.

"Billy Graham says that there are three things that will sideline a man of God faster than anything else: money, fame, and sex. And I think he's absolutely right," I responded.

"Okay, but these are people who have preached against all these things. Some of these fallen soldiers are men who influenced *me* to follow Jesus Christ. They loved the Lord. They knew and believed the Scriptures. They are people who were filled with the Spirit and had the fruit to show it. What was missing?"

Then he said something that you don't hear often. "Better still, what can you tell me to keep me from falling away? To quit on the Lord and His Church scares me to death."

"Given all these other elements," I answered, "the advice I would give you is this: No matter how long you live; no matter how successful you are in the ministry; how prominent; how blessed of God you are—stay accountable."

Have you noticed how many of the people who are going morally astray today are either independent types, or people who stand alone at the top of their organizations—in both cases, people who essentially answer to no one? Being alone and uncorrectable is a path which is littered with apostasy and unrighteousness.

Tragically, one of the best places on earth to insure spiritual autonomy is in our churches. Even though the pastor himself may be righteous and godly, so often he stops short of exercising His God-ordained care and directiveness for his people. Such an atmosphere promotes spiritual individualism and is a blatant mark of apostasy in the Body of Christ.

A SPIRITUAL MATTER

I have a friend who returned not long ago from an evangelistic mission among several churches in Australia. His account of what he learned opened a whole new vista of understanding for me.

He told of a certain attitude, a spirit, that prevailed among the churches he was with which had held back many people from being as fruitful for Christ as they should be. But it was more than simply an individual attitude among Christians. It was cultural—even national—in scope. It had to do with the way many of the people viewed themselves.

"In the midst of the campaign," he told a group of us, "the Holy Spirit began to speak to us about the root of the problem. It had to do with the very foundations of Australia. You know, this continent was settled by people who were offcasts from Great Britain—criminals, murderers, thieves, adulterers, and social misfits of all sorts.

"God impressed us with the fact that there is still a lingering spirit of rejection and worthlessness present among these people. They even bring it over into their Christian lives. Thus, when they go to worship God or bear witness for Christ, they are hampered by a horrible self-image, stemming from their past. You wouldn't believe how, once we began to speak to this matter and deal with it through the power of the Holy Spirit, the atmosphere cleared up, and the entire course of the meetings changed. But, to bring that change about, we had to come frontally against the spirit of rejection.

"When we got back to the United States, I related this experience to a close friend. It was as though we both caught the implications of it at the same time. Whereas the spirit of rejection permeates the Australian Church, so the spirit of independence dominates American Christians. Why is it that the American Church seems constantly to be fighting and losing in this battle of spiritual individualism? I believe it goes right back to our religious and national foundations.

"The founders of our nation left their homelands three hundred years ago over two basic issues: to escape political bondage and to gain religious freedom. The theme of it all was *independence.* They wanted to be independent spiritually and governmentally. And this has been the pervasive spirit of our nation ever since. Until we come against the spirit of independence that frolics through our American churches and our individual attitudes, our people will keep right on being accountable to no one."

I believe this assessment to be right on target. We have independence individualism built into our very fiber. The attitude that "nobody's going to tell me what to do" is an ingrained part of the American way of life.

Such independence, however, must never be allowed into our Christian walk. It is godless. It will keep on putting out the flames of renewal that are again present in our midst. It thwarts our witness to the world and runs counter to the Kingdom of God. And it is unholy to the core. One is reminded of the account of the rebellion and fall of Satan in Isaiah chapter 14, where five times Satan defiantly says, "I will," asserting himself against the plan of God.

> ... I will ascend into heaven, I will exalt my throne above the stars of God: I will sit also upon the mount of the congregation, in the sides of the north: I will ascend above the heights of the clouds; I will be like the most High.
>
> vs. 13, 14

In contrast to Satan's rebellion and arrogance, consider the holy and righteous attitude of our Lord Jesus Christ, who, when faced with death itself, proclaimed to His Father, "... nevertheless not My will, but Yours, be done" (Luke 22:42).

Holiness and accountability to godly authority go hand in hand. Remember, in conversion to Christ, one transfers kingdoms. We are delivered from the kingdom of darkness and transferred to the Kingdom of God's beloved Son (Colossians 1:13). One does not move from an independent state of sin to an independent state of righteousness. Instead, we are taken out of the government of darkness, headed up by Satan and his emissaries, and are translated into the government of God, reigning on earth today under the authority of the Father and the Son and the Holy Spirit in the Church. To put it another way, Bob Dylan is right: You've gotta serve somebody! Whether we are in sin or in righteousness, we are never there alone.

This is why the writer of Hebrews is so careful to warn his readers, "Obey those who have the rule over you, and submit yourselves, for they watch out for your souls ..." (Hebrews 13:17). Notice here that not only are Christians in general to be accountable, but that the leaders are called upon to be accountable people as well. That is why it is so utterly dangerous to follow authority that is under no authority. All of us who are truly in the Body of Christ are accountable.

THE BIBLICAL PATTERN

The way all of this worked in the New Testament Church is indeed a masterpiece painted by God, and the sort of accountability that was maintained there is something we sorely need to gain back in our own midst in the twentieth century.

Our Lord Jesus Christ gave authority to the Twelve to preach the Gospel and build the Church, and they passed on this authority to others. The first instance of their doing so is recorded in Acts 6, on the occasion of the ordination of the first seven deacons. As the Church grew, her governmental and service needs grew with her, and the Apostles responded accordingly.

It was only a matter of time until elders had been appointed in every Church (Acts 14:23). The Apostles continued to oversee the Churches but they settled more and more into territories. Indeed, by the time of the Jerusalem council described in Acts 15, James, "the brother of the Lord," who was not one of the twelve, is the bishop of that city. The Church historian Eusebius records extensive data about the episcopacy of James, known as James the Just.[9] That *bishop* is an early title for the Apostles is apparent from the fact that after the apostasy and death of Judas, Matthias was chosen to be numbered with the Twelve with the prophetic word, " . . . and his bishoprick let another take" (Acts 1:20 KJV). Embarrassing to most all modern translations, the Greek word in this passage is just plain *episkiope.*

By approximately A.D. 70, Ignatius had been consecrated Bishop of Antioch, and here we are still in the very center of New Testament times. His own letters, written about A.D. 107, recognize the presence of bishops, elders, and deacons in all of the Churches. In his letter to the Ephesians, Ignatius declares, "The bishops who have been appointed throughout the world exist by the purpose of Jesus Christ."[10] His letters, combined with the canonical letters of Paul to Timothy and Titus, accentuate how accountability was at work practically and visibly within the Body of Christ. It was *these* holy ones, we are reminded, who turned the world upside down. Christian people in the early centuries gave incredible obedience and allegiance to the bishops. The thought of living otherwise was foreign to their thinking. Accountability was in, independence was out, and the Church grew and prospered. But today things have changed, and the question inevitably arises, "What happens when the bishop himself goes sour?" Indeed, this has happened all too often throughout Church history. The answer is encouragingly simple.

The bishop was himself accountable to his neighboring bishops. Thus, if you felt a bishop had gone astray, you had a court of appeal to the bishops in the neighboring cities. And there are accounts in the history of the Early Church of unholy bishops being called into account, and sometimes being deposed. Certainly I do not mean by this that all things functioned perfectly. But what is apparent is that accountability was present in all levels of Church government, thereby carrying out the biblical injunction "that you also submit to such, and to everyone who works with us and labors" (1 Corinthians 16:16).

THE RISK OF BEING ACCOUNTABLE

I believe that it is in large part because of the spirit of independence bred into all of us, that we instantly rebel against the idea of being people who are answerable in the Body of Christ. As one extremist said recently, "If one thousand Spirit-filled elders believed it was God's will for me to move to Atlanta, and I didn't want to do it, I wouldn't budge."

Such rebellious attitudes polarize people into thinking that when it comes to accountability, there are absolutely two choices and two choices only: either being robots or being independent. The fact is, being accountable is neither.

Accountability is recognizing that the Kingdom of God has form and leadership, and willingly calling ourselves to be answerable within the bounds of the godly authority which the Lord has established in His Church. But let's be clear about one thing—there are risks.

There will be times when those in charge in the Church err, possibly making an "honest mistake" or perhaps even willfully side-stepping God's will. In the case of the latter, our whole cultural breeding instructs us to walk away, leaving that authority behind. But being holy gives us another option, for we are not conformed to the culture, but to the righteousness of Christ. Every possible effort should be made to communicate with those Church officials to whom the erring one is accountable, to seek correction. Even if correction cannot be satisfactorily obtained, in many cases the godly ones have been in history called upon by the Lord to stay on and continue walking by faith.

Think of the classic illustration of Moses and the spies back in the Old Testament. You will recall that in Numbers, chapter 13, the Lord instructed Moses: "Send thou men, that they may search the land of Canaan, which I give unto the children of Israel . . ." (v. 2). In response to this command, Moses chose twelve men, one from each of the twelve tribes, to go up into the land of Canaan and look the situation over. Numbered among the twelve were our two heroes, Joshua and Caleb.

When the committee reported back to Moses and Aaron, the vote was ten against and two for. Siding with the ten was the entire congregation of Israel, who were by this time weeping and tearing out their hair by the fistfuls over what would happen to them in moving into this strange new territory. Only Joshua and Caleb were willing to follow the Lord into this new terrain.

Though Moses interceded for the people, and the Lord forgave them, He forbade them to enter the land—promising entrance to their children instead. Think of the position of Joshua and Caleb! Though the Lord promised them entrance into the land, they had to go through forty years of wandering, homeless, with their faithless contemporaries.

What frightens me about the independent spirit in contemporary Christendom is, if you and I had been Joshua and Caleb, we'd have said something like this to Moses: "That does it! I've had it up to here. This covenant thing, this business of loyalty, only goes so far. From here on out, you're operating with two less spies." And we would have gone out and begun the Children of Israel Reorganized, or some other such thing.

But not so with Joshua and Caleb. Bless them, even though they knew they had done the Lord's will, rather than to rebel against the authority God had placed over them, they chose instead to remain obedient to Moses. That obedience was rewarded. Joshua was placed in charge at Moses' death, and God paid one of the highest compliments to Caleb that could ever be said of any man, as found in Numbers 14:24:

> But my servant Caleb, *because he had another spirit with him,* and hath followed me fully, him will I bring into the land whereinto he went; and his seed shall possess it [italics mine].

Let me ask a question. When it comes to accountability, whose spirit do you have? The spirit of answering to no one? Or the spirit of Caleb, who obeyed the Lord, kept himself accountable, *even though he was right and all Israel was wrong,* and ultimately received on earth the blessing of God?

THE PLACE WHERE WE ANSWER

The question then becomes, where is it that I am to be answerable? Plainly and simply, it is in the Church. Ultimately, of course, all of us will stand before the judgment seat of Christ, but until that time, the place where we give an account is before God's appointed authorities in His Church.

But, you ask, "What if I get an 'Israel'?" Let me ask a question in return. Was Israel God's chosen people? Yes, it was. And if you are waiting around for the world's perfect church in which to be accountable, you will probably end up following yourself. For this is where the spirit of independence ends up. Being accountable carries risk. But I promise you, in being alone and independent, the risks are far greater.

I have a close friend who went through perhaps one of the most dramatic Christian pilgrimages in this area of accountability and authority that I have ever heard told.

He began in a huge Protestant denomination, which is generally noted for being dead, or at best, sleepy. His own congregation was quite alive to the things of Christ, but when the call came for him to enter the Christian ministry, he left that drowsy denomination to look for something more vital. The next denomination he entered was smaller and seemed to have a bit more zip. But, after several years of service there, he found that liberalism and lethargy were crouching at the door with ever-more imposing presence, and it was not long before he left this jurisdiction for one of the large parachurch organizations. After eight years of service in it, successful to all outward appearances, but hungry for worship and community which only a true Church can provide, he left to join a newly formed church. In this new situation, the man in charge gradually, but steadily, embraced some of the subtle heresies long rejected by Christendom. Seeing the error, my friend left this group after eighteen months, and was now virtually alone.

The story got my attention when he said to me one day, "I realized that I could split yet once more. For being alone is not as splintered as one can get. The final split is when you split from yourself. They call it schizophrenia. And I realized that, unless I brought my life back under the lordship of Christ and His Church, this is exactly where I was headed."

Today this man enjoys a fruitful ministry, right back in the historic Christian faith where he started. And you won't find a stronger proponent for true Christian unity. His days of independence have come to a glorious end.

Conservative Baptist Church historian Bruce Shelley says it well in *The Church: God's People:*

> Believers need to see that the Church is part and parcel of true salvation, just as marriage is inextricably linked to true love. To love truly, one assumes responsibility for the loved one. That is marriage. To be saved truly, one is added to a body of saved ones. That is the Church. . . . While saving faith is an intensely personal matter, it is never purely a private matter.

The simple truth is, as long as we continue on our merry way of private religion, we may as well write off the possibility of experiencing true righteousness, or of changing the hearts of men and nations for Christ. Just as a good soldier does not fight without his army, so we cannot overturn the powers of darkness alone. If we continue to make saving faith private, making it strictly a matter between the individual and God, with the Church only an interested bystander, we will see unholiness prosper, and our last state will be worse than the first.

With singleness of purpose, our Lord Jesus Christ has raised up one place and one place only for His holy ones to call home, a place in which they can be accountable and answerable. But if the Church is it, why then are there today so many other agencies and gospel gimmicks, which call for our allegiance? Author Walter J. Chantry assesses our situation well in his book *God's Righteous Kingdom:*

Freelance men "serve the Lord" with complete comfort in their isolation from the Church. All manner of agencies arise to spread the gospel, exalt the Lord, and bring in the Kingdom while they shun the Church. How the gospel may be detached from the Church, how the Lord has come to be separated from the Church, and how Kingdom and Church are now so diverse, they can never explain.

And then Chantry goes on to say:

> It is so easy to claim that one's society is "the right arm of the Church," but as a matter of fact, some agencies feed on the Church only to attack the Church. Organizations draw the strongest sons of the Church away from her. They use the Church to raise funds to promote their influence and to recruit their forces. Little is ever given in return to the Church. If this bleeding of the Church is questioned, agencies snap back that after all they are more effective in serving Christ than the Churches. Here their true attitude is revealed. They think the real activity of the Spirit today is in societies outside the Church. But Jesus has not yet announced a divorce of His Bride![11]

In a day when "Christian Work" is so widely substituted for the Church, it is crucial for us to see that our accountability to Christ is intended to be within the framework of His Body. It is for the *Church* that He will one day return to this earth for a second time. Not to be found within her gates is a far greater gamble than to chance accountability to her.

In the last half-century or so, we have had our fling with every sort of parachurch agency imaginable. The fallouts from this emphasis have produced massive disenchantment in the lives of people who have served under men who gave virtually no account at all. But they have attracted the followers. As a matter of fact, where are all the gifted young theologians today? You are hard pressed to name many in the Church. Most of them are in the parachurch movements. How about the effective communicators and speakers? Or the Bible teachers? They are filling the ranks of all sorts of religious societies—organizations that promised they would feed the Church, but have not.

It is time for the holy people of God to once again commit themselves to Him in the Church. If you are a parachurch worker, I urge you: Make the shift back to using your gifts in the Church. If you are a student considering a Christian vocation, come on back home to the Body of Christ and serve Him there.

Our holiness and godliness are deeply affected by whether or not we are accountable people. And where we are accountable is crucial to both as well. May we steadfastly resist the spirit of independence at every turn, and hear the Spirit and the Bride say, "Come."

9
The Sanctification of Time

We follow the clock and the calendar around, brothers and sisters, from prayer-time to prayer-time, from feast to feast. More than that, we advance year to year, from this year's fast to next year's, from this year's holiday to next year's holiday. So as the year has moved around, the time has come once again for a new beginning—this year's announcement of the blessed Passover, the date on which our Lord was sacrificed.[12]

Up to this point, we have talked almost exclusively about the holiness of God, people, and things. At this juncture, we want to turn our attention toward a subject which you may not have thought of as being related to the theme of holiness: *time*.

In a major speech early in his presidency, John F. Kennedy said pointedly, "Time is not our friend." I didn't want to admit it, but this was true in my own life. Though equipped with a calendar watch, a Seven-Star Diary, a year-at-a-glance notebook, and a day-to-day personal schedule, which I had devised, time somehow still worked against me. Hours ran into days, days into weeks, weeks into months and years, and though I was organized, there was something wrong with the way I was making my journey through time.

All of us know only too well how evasive time is. It so easily slips through our fingers, and ends up getting the best of us. Do you find yourself rushed, hurried, late, behind, swamped, and tied up? You're not alone, but life doesn't have to be this way. God has a better program for time.

Although He transcends time in a realm called eternity, God does not sidestep time. He works in and through time. It was He who created time, for in the opening verses of the Holy Scripture, we see time established in the very Creation itself. Time is, therefore, a vital element in our consideration here, for it is an integral part of God's program for a holy people, and for stability even in the world.

SUNRISE, SUNSET

Mark it well: People who view their time as set apart to the Lord will make strong gains on getting control of their clocks and calendars. And, as with other matters related to holiness, we do not sanctify our schedules for our own benefit. Rather, we set our hours, days, weeks, and years apart to the Lord for His glory. God has in His written Word given us an amazing amount of instruction, which the Church has wholeheartedly entered into over the centuries.

In the beginning, God established the time frame we know as a *day*. Originally, *day,* as used in Genesis, chapter 7, had reference to that period of time between sunrise and sunset, called in this passage *morning* and *evening*. God the Father, together with His Son and His Holy Spirit, created the earth and all its creatures during the course of six days. On the seventh day, God rested.

Already, before we are even one chapter into the Scriptures, we encounter two specific units of time: the day and the week. We see God communing with Adam on a daily basis, and we are told how God has set apart the seventh day for rest.

But by the time of the Exodus, the concept of the holy year is also fully engrained within the culture of Israel. As a matter of fact, its very first mention in the Scripture has to do with the establishment of sanctified time as related to the Passover: the setting apart unto God of one week out of the year for the people to remember their deliverance from Egypt. Note in Exodus 13:6–10 the mention of the day, the week, and the year, all three.

Seven days thou shalt eat unleavened bread, and in the seventh day shall be a feast to the Lord.

Unleavened bread shall be eaten seven days; and there shall no leavened bread be seen with thee, neither shall there be leaven seen with thee in all thy quarters.

And thou shalt shew thy son in that day, saying, This is done because of that which the Lord did unto me when I came forth out of Egypt.

And it shall be for a sign unto thee upon thine hand, and for a memorial between thine eyes, that the Lord's law may be in thy mouth: for with a strong hand hath the Lord brought thee out of Egypt.

Thou shalt therefore keep this ordinance in his season from year to year.

And so, added to the Feast of Unleavened Bread, which was already being observed, the Passover is the second annual observance in Israel. Before long, God would have His nation living its entire year centered around signposts of time, dealing with worship of and obedience to Him. Time was never to be a passing thing for the people of God. Spontaneity has not been the rule of life. Instead, holy people have lived by the Lord's command that definite periods of time within the year be set apart for worship, fasting, feasting, and celebration.

Thus, we see that there is—in the broadest possible sense—a *liturgy* of time. There is pattern in the way God governs time. He causes it to progress and move forward, and we are in it and take part in it. Our participation also has a format—regular and cyclical.

As we read through the Scriptures, it is impossible to escape the sense of time-rightness in events. These fall where they should, for God has ordained them there. The psalmist writes, "My times are in thy hand . . ." (Psalms 31:15). Paul tells us that "when the fullness of the time had come, God sent forth His Son . . ." (Galatians 4:4). And the ordering and the spacing of the events of our salvation, with our lives falling at their appointed time, is clearly established by God. That you, personally, are on the scene this moment, partaking in Christ's salvation, is in no way mere chance.

Human beings have not, however, always accepted God's ordering of their lives in time. Mankind has consistently rushed down the corridor of time, ignoring God's order of setting apart time, and trying to put their own meaning into it. Secularizing time, they have attempted to build for themselves a sense of their *own* history and their *own* place, independent of His plan.

It is in time that God seeks men, and it is in time that men turn away from Him. But for the holy ones, for those who have come under the active reign of the Lord Jesus Christ in His Holy Church, there is incredible security in knowing that our place in time *relates* to all of the past and of the future—yes, even to eternity. All of the events in that short space of time from birth to physical death are meant to fit precisely into God's matrix of time.

Even the bad times!

And just as Israel of old walked through a cyclical year that was set apart to God and for Him, the same has always been, and is now, true with respect to the Church as well. That fact is a shock to some, because we live in an age in which the meaning of the yearly cycle has been ignored or forgotten. This loss is not limited only to secular society. The Church, too, by and large, has lost the meaning of its year—and with it, that indispensable experience of eternity in time.

THE COMMON CALENDAR

But wait a minute! It's not that there is no cyclical year, for everyone has a cycle of the year. The question really is: Are we on God's cycle or man's? The common calendar or the holy calendar? The secular world certainly has its annual pattern, its special handling of the calendar. Let's look at it for a moment.

The pagan year begins on New Year's Day, with a tremendous headache and the liturgy of the Bowls: Sugar, Cotton, Rose, and Orange. We talk about a "new beginning" with the changing of the calendar on the wall—but it never comes. For mere numbers change nothing. People anticipated a fresh start again this year, but it did not happen.

With his nonbeginning on New Year's Day, the citizen of the secular world looks forward to certain other holidays, and to being off work. Lincoln's and Washington's birthdays, now reduced to Presidents' Day, offer a short break from the monotony of nine to five. For those in love, Valentine's Day is a pleasant opportunity for candy, cards, and flowers. But for the lonely, the unloved, or out-of-love, Valentine's Day offers little.

Big on the East Coast and in our larger cities is the day when everyone wears something green, and grown-ups sip green drinks and eat green food—Saint Patrick's Day. The world has swiped this one from us. For this is the day which commemorates the son of a Christian deacon in Britain, back in the fifth century, who at sixteen was captured by Irish marauders and made a slave. It was at this time he was converted to Christ. He writes, "The Lord opened to me my unbelief that I might remember my sins and that I might return with my whole heart to the Lord my God."

Later Saint Patrick escaped, probably to Britain, and in a vision, God called him to return to Ireland with the glorious Gospel of Christ. He was trained, sent out by the Church, became an apostle·

to Ireland. He broke through heathenism to evangelize the country and to establish the Church. But today, even most Irish-Americans have forgotten the significance of his day and have but the vaguest sense of Saint Patrick's holy work.

Then there's another break in the schedule—"spring break," they call it now—at or near what Christians call Easter. There's usually a long weekend, maybe even a whole week, to get away on a quick trip to one of those Florida beaches to lie on the sand, listen to music, and watch the girls go by.

Next comes a day promoted by various florists' associations, which has strangely found its way into the liturgical calendars of many independent churches: Mother's Day. It usually means Sunday dinner out and a corsage for a deserving mom, and maybe even a family-oriented message from the pulpit.

Then, Memorial Day rolls around. For some, Memorial Day means more than a vacation, for there is the memory of the dearly departed who have given their lives for their country. For others, it's another of those holidays of debauchery, an excuse to get away from it all. Severe sunburns often keep the memory of the weekend alive a day or two extra. And at last—school is out.

From here on there's nothing much to look forward to until the Fourth of July. For some, Independence Day is the celebration of the birth of the nation. For others, it's simply firecrackers and picnics in the city parks. For most, the "Fourth" is just another lost weekend: four days of beer, booze, and binge. But at least summer has come. We can play in the sun and build up our tans. There are backyard barbecues, outdoor tennis, swimming, and drives in the country.

The days come and go. August is here, hot and "muggy." Summer's almost gone. "Dog days," we call them. And it's suddenly almost fall. Back to school again. And that last big holiday of the summer is here—Labor Day. Not much "labor" to it, really, unless you call popping the tab on the aluminum can *labor*.

But wait—there's more anticipation. For Halloween is near. And soon it will be Thanksgiving, the big feast when all the family comes home; Grandma fixes turkey; Aunt Susie bakes the pumpkin pie, and everyone eats too much. The ladies clean up the kitchen, the men watch the TV game of the day, and the children play.

Religious or not, the biggest event of the year is now just around the corner—Christmas. I wonder what *I'll* get? What are my friends and relatives going to give *me* this year? And then the year draws to a close on New Year's Eve, when everyone goes out and gets loaded. Again.

Isn't this really Everyman's typical calendar, always giving him something to look forward to? Of course it is, because he has got to order time and take breaks from his schedule. Certainly he has a cycle. The monotony without it would drive him crazy. But, it is a dismal cycle at best. For the pattern takes us nowhere. It is timed by man and for man. And even those who are captured by it will usually admit that it ends up a disappointment. Another year without meaning.

And most certainly, this secular cycle does not even come close in measuring up at all to the yearly cycle of the Church of the living God.

THE HOLY CALENDAR

The Church has, as we have said, its own year: sacred, holy, and, yes, cyclical. You may have heard some people pooh-pooh the idea of regular, set holy days, or even condemn the notion. You will run into a Christian now and then who naively interprets Paul's warnings against new moons, sabbaths, and holy days (Colossians 2:16-23) as a statement against having a Church calendar. They woefully misread him, however. His warnings are against Christians returning to Jewish observances, and must not be twisted to apply to the holy days of the Christian Church. To do so not only stretches his words out of context, but abuses the leading of the Holy Spirit in the Church through the ages. It would be like taking the passage "Much learning is driving you mad!" (Acts 26:24), and using it to discredit Christian education. The substance of our relationship with Christ must be experienced in time, and the Church calendar is God's means of keeping our experience in the cycle of the year sacred.

The historic Church Year begins with our celebration of the coming of the Lord Jesus Christ. Advent means to "come to," and this season commemorates the coming of the eternal Son of the Father to earth. It is "for us men and for our salvation" that He became flesh. As we relive our drama of anticipation, we remember His First Coming and yearn for His return at the close of the age. In the West, the Advent season begins four Sundays before Christmas and continues through Christmas Day. During this season, the Church has always devoted itself to the reading of the Scriptures, which tell of the Incarnation of our Lord Jesus Christ and of His Second Coming.

The pinnacle of Advent, of course, is Christmas Day, our celebration of the earthly birth of the Son of God. Second only to Easter as a holy day among God's people, Christmas is a fulfillment of our deepest expectations, as we enter into the joy of the Lord coming to man. Some people—occasionally, even sincere Christians—will denounce Christmas as having its roots in a pagan holiday. They feel the Church has been duped into celebrating Jesus' earthly birth on December 25, and that having a Christmas tree and giving gifts is a misleading hoax of history.

Such a view generally comes from a misunderstanding of how the Church views time. You see, at stake here is the whole concept of the *sanctification of time,* setting time apart from common use for the Lord. The fact is, December 25 *was* a pagan holiday. But no longer. For God's people said, in effect, "Let's take it over for the Lord and make it holy." Very consciously, our forebears in the faith, sometime in the early fourth century, captured December 25 from their pagan opponents. They declared it instead to be the date on which the birth from Mary of our Lord Jesus Christ would be commemorated. Did they succeed?

To this very day, Christmas is celebrated worldwide. Commercialism attacks it, the American Civil Liberties Union hauls the singing of its hymns by schoolchildren into our courts, and people miss its meaning. But on it goes. The witness to Christ is established. Who among us can even so much as name the pagan event which the Church snuffed out? I love it! Such a retaking of time represents a great victory for Christ and His Kingdom. It's called *changing the world!*

And our year continues. We come to January 6, the day called Epiphany, which means *appearance.* We celebrate Christ's revelation to the world as the Son of God, and with it, His baptism to fulfill all righteousness. The Orthodox Church retains the ancient practice of the pastors coming to each home in the Church to bless it in the name of the Lord for the year ahead. How sorely we Christians need the blessing of God on our homes and families in these trying times! Somehow, as we forget these practices, these time sanctifiers, we forget the Lord as well. Could it be that one reason the devourer captures so many of our homes is that we have failed to keep them sanctified to the Lord?

Now, as the Church Year progresses, we see up ahead those events surrounding the Lord's Passion. Since very, very early days, the Church has taken a period of time to give attention to Christ's suffering and to what it would have meant to be without Him. And that forty-day period preceding Easter, called Lent, is a time of solemn preparation for the celebration of Christ's Resurrection, recognizing ourselves to be people who did not deserve His Crucifixion and His Resurrection on our behalf. During this time some believers engage in some form of fast, some abstinence which helps direct their hearts toward the meaning of the season.

Saint Augustine writes concerning the Lenten season of his day:

> For as these days succeed in regular season, with a joyful cheerfulness, the past days of Lent, whereby the misery of this life before the Resurrection of the Lord's body is signified; so that day which after the Resurrection shall be given to the full body of the Lord, that is to the Holy Church, when all the troubles and sorrows of this life have been shut out, shall succeed with perpetual bliss. But this life demandeth from us self-restraint, that although groaning and weighed down with our toil and struggles, and desiring to be clothed upon with our house which* is from heaven, we may refrain from secular pleasures—and this is signified by the number of forty, which was the period of the fasts of Moses and Elijah, and of our Lord Himself.[13]

For us, the events highlighted in our Church Year are not just days to be marked off on the calendar. Christ is our Lord, and we live the days of our lives in continual recognition of that fact. Though the general populace may acclaim Him and yet not want Him as Lord; though American civil religion condescends to honor Him without recognizing His Lordship; we who are His Church approach Palm Sunday committed, abandoned, and consecrated to the One who came to die. Finally, we enter Holy Week with hearts truly sorry for sin, fasting from Thursday night till Sunday.

In my church we receive communion on the evening of Maundy Thursday. Then we fast, eating only a meal of soup and bread on Friday evening and again on Saturday evening, until the Great Eucharist on Easter Sunday morning. Most of us feel discomfort during these days, and some of us are *very* uncomfortable. Bothersome headaches may come, and people often do not sleep very well. Even the discomfort, however, contributes to the joy of the faithful.

Fasting is a voluntary sacrifice of the satisfaction of the desires of the body. In it, there is a sense of being with Christ in His suffering and, in the case of Holy Week, looking to the Resurrection. People who fast look forward to Easter Sunday with great anticipation. You *experience* a portion of the Lord's suffering when you enter into such a time of fasting; so you know why and with whom you are hurting. And after the suffering comes the victory, for His Resurrection means *our* resurrection. In the historic Church the Great Eucharist of Easter was followed by a feast of celebration with the entire congregation present.

Among God's people there has always been both fasting and feasting. Fasting is what makes feasting seem so good! By contrast, the world doesn't get all that much satisfaction out of the Thanksgiving Day feast. People have been eating well all along—at least here in America—right? Our stomachs aren't all that small. But, after a fast, the taste of abundant food is an occasion of joy—with the giving of thanks. Most of all, however, the feasts of the Church are an extension of communion and a foretaste of the Marriage Supper of the Lamb. Even the abundant food aspect of the feast is not there because of gluttony, but because we celebrate with our Lord and look forward to the ultimate heavenly celebration.

Historically, a period of feasting in the Church runs from Easter to Pentecost—a week of Sundays: Easter Sunday and the following six Sundays. From Easter to Pentecost, nobody fasts. Instead, we celebrate that which we, along with the ancient Christians experience: the Lord Jesus Christ resurrected in our midst.

Forty days after Easter, another great event takes place: Ascension. And we celebrate the initiation of the reign of the Son. Then, on Pentecost Sunday, there is more jubilation, because of the coming of the Holy Spirit to the Church. Can you imagine anything more frustrating than being grateful beyond words for the gift of the Holy Spirit, and having no vehicle through which to offer up praise and thanksgiving? Listen—our Churches need to activate the Feast of Pentecost again! No wonder our zealots are going to Holiday Inn for shouting suppers on Saturday nights. The Church has forgotten to celebrate Pentecost!

The longest period of the Church Year, from Pentecost to Advent, is the time in which the Church lives out her pilgrimage in the world, with the Holy Spirit as her strength, utilizing His gifts, receiving His teaching and His guidance into all truth. It is the season of the Church Militant, the time during which God's people serve as the active priesthood of Jesus Christ, in a world which needs Him so desperately.

Why has the Church recognized a *special* season of militancy? Aren't we to be "combat ready" at all times in our service to the Lord?

To the second question, the answer is *yes.* The crucial answer to the first question is that when people are militant *all* the time, they wear out and they quit. When there's no specific time set aside for militancy, only the Christian activists are ever militant. Besides that, militant is not everything we are to be. Far more foundational, we are to be a *worshiping* people. Our Church Year is centered around worship, the sanctification of our time, and consequently our own sanctification.

Remember that last go-get-'em evangelism seminar that was held at your church? And all the people who responded to the invitation at the end to be aggressive witnesses for Christ? Let me ask: How many stuck with it? And of those who lasted, how many are carrying on with joy?

There is a great lesson we can learn here from our fellow believers in the Church of the past. Rather than trying to be continually militant, how about five months a year? Utilize the months from Pentecost to Advent for aggressive evangelism, special programs of ministry to the poor, certain neighborhood projects, and all the rest. Then, from Advent to Pentecost again—all the while being available to the Holy Spirit for whatever opportunity for outreach or service presents itself—God's people can be about such things as personal spiritual inventory, deepening the heart's love for Christ, devotional reading, fasting, feasting, and the worship of God.

Even during the season of militancy, there are signposts along the way. We celebrate the mystery of the Holy Trinity on the first Sunday after Pentecost, for we worship Father, Son, and Holy Spirit. Finally, at the end of the season on the last Sunday before Advent, we celebrate Christ as King. For He has been, is, and will be our King forever. And the year once again is brought to a glorious close.

Can you see why the Church Year must be regained as a vital part of the personal and corporate life of the people of God? It is the only way we have to truly sanctify time, to set each year apart to

God, and keep it consecrated all year long. Admittedly, regaining it and keeping it holy will be difficult. We live in an age which has forgotten what making time holy is all about—an age in which, even for the Church, these days are just historic events on a calendar of the past. Personally, I am committed to the proposition that our generation can regain the Church Year, and experience the glory of it, as our predecessors in the faith once did.

The English theologian Richard Hooker viewed the Church calendar as a means of both edification and evangelism.

> Well to celebrate these religious and sacred days is to spend the flower of our time happily. They are the splendor and outward dignity of our religion, forcible witnesses of ancient truth, provocation to the exercise of all piety, shadows of our endless felicity in heaven, on earth everlasting records and memorials, wherein they who cannot be drawn down to hearken to what we teach, nay, only by looking on what we do, in a manner read whatsoever we believe.[14]

Some may say, "The repetition of the year over and over again will become monotonous and boring." Remember, however, that in pagan life, the liturgy of the year is repeated over and over again. Frankly, you cannot escape repetition—nor would you want to. Uncertainty is far more devastating than monotony. Our choices are essentially the world's calendar or the Church's calendar. We must take one or the other. Without a proper view of the year, we can forget the sanctification of time. And when our *time* structure is not given over to God, it's far more difficult for our *lives* to be set apart to Him.

Be encouraged. Repetition is the mother of learning. In repeating what is true, you participate in a deeper level in the things of God; for repetition makes present what the Lord has done for us and enables us to relive His acts of grace year by year.

SETTING APART THE WEEK

So, our year, a glorious year, continues in continuity with the centuries past, on through to the present and into the future, until the Second Advent of our Lord Jesus Christ. But years are also made up of smaller intervals called "weeks." And the weeks repeat as well—do they not?

We might say that for the pagan Everyman, the week consists of
going to work on Monday, returning home to watch TV and go to
bed; getting up Tuesday morning, going to work, coming home,
watching TV, and going to bed—until Friday. Ah, yes, *Friday!*
Here is the zenith of seven days, the highest day of the unsanctified
week, because it ushers in the weekend. For it is here that the good
times start. Television promises us that "weekends were made for
Michelob." But, in reality, things usually do not work out all that
well.

Unless you are holy, pleasures simply do not last. The world cannot deliver on its promises. The secular week is a giant letdown,
isn't it! Sunday evening rolls around, and you cannot bring yourself
to look forward to Monday. "Blue Monday," it is often called. But
Monday comes anyway, and already people start looking ahead to
Friday. I know. I did it for years. Thus beginneth that now famous
slogan known as *TGIF.*

But for the people of God, the whole of the week fits in with our
life in Christ. Each week constitutes a cycle which we hold sacred.
For time itself is sacred for us. As the ancient liturgy says, "Holy
things are for the holy."

We, too, live through the trials and tribulations of daily life—
getting up, going to work, coming back home, engaging in evening
activity, and retiring. And for us, too, it is sometimes monotonous.
Even humdrum. But there's a majestic difference. In union with
Christ, we live as His priesthood. We move among the people of the
world, knowing who and what we are, and to what we have been
called.

We come from the worship of God on Sunday, our first day of the
week, and we step out into the world with His benediction—the
people of God sent forth to labor. And we are not alone; we are together, sharing our common sanctified week, though we may work
with none but non-Christians.

Throughout the week we anticipate the coming Sunday, and perhaps we pause again during the week to come together at a mid-
week or vesper service. When the week is past, we return to feast at
the Lord's banquet, gathering in the Heavenly Holy of Holies to
present that once-for-all offering, provided for us in Christ, gaining
life from His body and His blood, entering into His rest. From this
rest, we go again to face the world, but not alone, not just as individuals. For we are bone of His bone and flesh of His flesh; in union
with Christ, and through Him related to one another.

Thus, each week is sanctified, filled with work and anticipation, fulfillment and rest.

THE SANCTIFIED DAY

Finally, each week is filled with seven smaller time intervals we call *days*. Every day, too, holds a cycle for us.

Historically, both in Israel and in the Church, there have been appointed hours for regular prayer. We have essentially forgotten to pray during the hustle-bustle of the modern age. Some individuals have sought out ways of having their own "quiet times." But, historically, the Church together, engaged in prayer at appointed times, just as had Israel before her; the *whole* of the congregation of the Lord took part in prayer. And it had to do with sanctifying the day, setting it apart to God.

In Psalms 55:17, we read from King David, "Evening and morning, and at noon, I will pray, and cry aloud: and he shall hear my voice." Besides daily worship, we also get to fuss a bit.

Daniel, too, prayed three times a day. For that was the custom in Israel, as we see in Daniel 6:10: "Now when Daniel knew that the writing was signed, he went into his house; and his windows being open in his chamber toward Jerusalem, he kneeled upon his knees three times a day, and prayed, and gave thanks before his God, as he did aforetime."

Traditionally, the Jewish prayers were at dawn, at noon, and at dusk. It seems very likely that most of those prayers were set prayers, content that had been used for centuries, in addition to specific petitions inserted because of the need in the hour, as in Daniel's case.

From its very inception, the Church followed the practice of Israel. This is made clear early in the Book of Acts, as we read chapter 3, verse 1. "Now Peter and John went up to the temple at the hour of prayer, the ninth hour."

And throughout history, the faithful have continued such hours of prayer. The great Reformer, Martin Luther, taught the necessity of prayer on rising and prayer on retiring at night. As part of those daily prayers, he specified the Lord's Prayer. That prayer, preceded by a short reading from the Scriptures, followed by a simple commitment of the day or night to the Lord, certainly forms an appropriate practice for those Christians today who wish to begin by sanctifying each day to the Lord.

YOUR TIME SANCTIFIED

All these practices—the keeping of holy days, the keeping of the week with its center upon the Eucharist, the sanctifying of the day—have their focus and meaning in a life oriented toward worship of Father, Son, and Holy Spirit. In such a life the pinnacle of each year is Easter, the celebration of the Resurrection of Christ; every Sunday is a repetition of that celebration; and the awakening of each new morning is an experience of the same.

For Christ is risen, "trampling down death by death."[15] Our whole life is one of anticipating and experiencing the coming of Christ into the world, His life among men, His death for us, His Resurrection, His reign in the Church, and His coming again. The Christ who is always with us (Matthew 28:20) will return for us (John 14:3). As long as we live on the earth, we live in the tension of these truths, remembering Him, experiencing His presence, expecting His return. To do so properly, we practice a daily, weekly, and yearly liturgy designed to sanctify our time, to set it apart and live it for Him.

And when it is made holy, time can be our friend.

10

Getting Ourselves in Gear

One huge question looms unanswered in the minds of many Christians today: How does bodily purity relate to holiness? What does it mean for your body to be "set apart to God"?

In some circles the question is avoided by simply laying out a few rules which have been humorously summarized by a bit of doggerel verse:

> Don't smoke, drink, dance or chew,
> Or run around with girls who do.

Rules to this effect have been written into the by-laws and covenants of many local churches in this country. Worse yet, such rules have been accepted by Christians as holding the biblical solutions to the problems surrounding bodily purity. In reality, they do nothing of the sort. For just giving people rules is a simplistic legalistic solution, which sweeps the matter of morality under the rug, without dealing with the real core issues.

The heart of bodily holiness is succinctly stated by Paul in the sixth chapter of his letter to the church of Rome. There, in the context of his discussion of our union with Christ, the great apostle writes, "Do not present your members as instruments of unrighteousness to sin, but present yourselves to God as being alive from the dead, and your members as instruments of righteousness to God" (Romans 6:13).

Here, then, we see the true focus of any approach to bodily purity or holiness: Dedicate the members of your body to God for His use. That is Paul's constant theme on the body, repeated over and over. Let's look for ourselves.

In 1 Corinthians 3:16:

> Do you not know that you are the temple of God and that the Spirit of God dwells in you?

In 1 Corinthians 6:13, 19:

> Foods for the stomach and the stomach for foods, but God will
> destroy both it and them. Now the body is not for sexual immo-
> rality but for the Lord, and the Lord for the body.

> Or do you not know that your body is the temple of the Holy
> Spirit who is in you, whom you have from God, and you are not
> your own?

In Romans 12:1:

> I beseech you therefore, brethren, by the mercies of God, that
> you present your bodies a living sacrifice, holy, acceptable to
> God, which is your reasonable service.

The emphasis the apostle Paul makes on sin and the body tells us
that bodily purity will require constant vigilance, and even warfare,
on our part. Purity is not a cakewalk, nor is it an automatic
by-product of Christ living in a passive heart. The Scriptures teach
otherwise.

We, relying upon our union with Christ and the power of the
Holy Spirit, must apply ourselves to "restraining and regulating the
appetites of the body so that they be in moderation and temper-
ance,"as Andrew Murray so aptly put it in *Holy in Christ.* That is
why we have some sympathy with those who made the rules we
mentioned earlier. They were simply engaged in a mistaken effort to
help Christians keep their bodies under control.

As part of the race of beings made in God's image, you may be
the clearest picture of Him the unbelieving world will ever see.
Thus, your imagery, your appearance, is incredibly important. It
relates both to bringing glory to God, and to showing the world that
the Gospel works for us in the way we keep ourselves.

Not all of us are good-looking, but all of us can look good. Looking good says to the rest of creation, "As custodian of this temple of
the Holy Spirit, I am giving priority to making sure I carefully rep-
resent the glory of God at the best possible level."

I don't know of anything more tragic than a run-down, lacklus-
ter, unkempt display case for the Holy Spirit to dwell in. Being
overweight is just one visible statement about who or what is truly

in control of your body. It is so easy to waltz with gluttony.

Author Karen Wise, who went from 340 pounds to a size 9 dress, writes in *God Knows—I Won't Be Fat Again:*

> There wasn't one area of my life that wasn't affected by my problem. I had been willing to accept second-best in order to eat ... I was a foodaholic. Food had precisely as much control over me as drugs have over an addict. It totally drained my worth as a person. My life was controlled by what I ate and by the fact that I couldn't quit.

Her turning point came when she brought her problem under the reign of Jesus Christ. She says, "If God isn't strong enough to win out over all you have been, all the disappointments you have lived through, all the weaknesses you still have, then He really isn't what you say He is."

And it's a warfare, isn't it? We can rationalize it: "Pray about it," and offer excuses. It is the will of God for us to forsake our alibis, and trim off the weight which so easily besets us.

For many people, severe weight problems can be traced back to unconfessed sin, to confusion about the true nature of forgiveness, and how it tangibly applies on such an issue as basic as this one. Lifelong habits of guilt and self-persecution, as they relate to what goes into our mouths, whether it be food, drugs, or alcohol, are issues that need to be examined closely and carefully by those in spiritual authority over you. We tend to lose wars like these by trying to go it alone.

This is why the proper place for us to forsake our alibis, to confess our sins to Christ, is in the Church. This is not a matter of self-diagnosis or self-medication. Christ, in His glorious wisdom, has given us a haven to regain and rebuild our health—physical as well as spiritual. Often, a brother or sister in Christ can be a "doctor of the spirit" to minister to us in these areas where our track record of success is nil. He has given us the "medicine of immortality," His holy feast, to assist us in our daily warfare against sin, death, and the devil. The fact is, in Christ we can bring our physical bodies under the care of the Great Physician, our Lord and Savior, Jesus Christ. It is part of our heritage in the Church.

But the same Paul cautions his readers against trusting man-made rules—which so readily backfire—in his letter to the Colossians, chapter 2, verses 20–23:

Therefore, if you died with Christ from the basic principles of the world, why, as though living in the world, do you subject yourself to regulations—

"Do not touch, do not taste, do not handle," which all concern things which perish with the using—according to the commandments and doctrines of men?

These things indeed have an appearance of wisdom in self-imposed religion, false humility, and neglect of the body—not of any value against the indulgence of the flesh.

No, the control of the body is not managed by rules, but by a consistent warfare, aided and abetted by a Church, which cares enough to put its time and effort on the line.

But the positive side of yielding our members to God is perhaps the greatest weapon of all. Paul's command was that we so yield our bodies, and it is clear that he had specifics in mind. Let us zero in on the use of three bodily members: hands, feet, and mouth. What sort of use might God intend for these?

THESE HANDS

Every move that we make says something; each gesture sends out a message. Several years ago, the best-selling book *Body Language* established very clearly the importance of such things as posture, proximity to another person, and how we use our arms and hands, which *communicate* how we feel or what we are trying to say.

While on the 1976 campaign trail, Vice-President Rockefeller dealt a serious blow to whatever political future he might have had, when, in response to a heckler, he "shot a bird" in the direction of his foe. A news photographer happened to be camera-ready at the exact instant, and snapped a picture for all of posterity to remember. News wires around the world carried the picture of the Vice-President using an obscene gesture to vent anger and frustration. And just as the "deleted expletives" of Richard Nixon were criticized—even by the world at large—so, too, such undignified use of the hands by a public official was viewed as improper.

By contrast, hands belonging to one set apart to the Lord are referred to in Scripture as "holy hands" (1 Timothy 2:8). Certainly there are many ways the hands are used that are common for both believers and unbelievers. All people use them for work, for play, for clapping, and for waving greetings. I'm not about to belittle such uses, for they are proper, and can even be holy.

But there are some acts that only a believer can do with real meaning. These particularly set apart holy hands from common hands. And as we view the use of our hands, it is these holy things which give us a feel for the fact of their dedication to the Lord. What are some examples?

1. With our hands we minister to the Lord. The human hands are the physical members of our bodies which carry out what our brains decide to do—be that act good or bad.

In Genesis, chapter 4, we read that after Cain slew his brother Abel, the Lord said to him in pronouncing judgment, "And now you are cursed from the ground, which has opened its mouth to receive your brother's blood from your *hand*" (*see* Genesis 4:11). In other words, the murder did not occur merely because Cain *decided* to do it; it occurred because he carried out that decision with his hands. Thus, his hands became the physical focal point of his guilt. This brings to mind Paul's statement in Romans: "I speak in human terms because of the weakness of your flesh. For just as you have presented your members as servants to uncleanness, and to lawlessness leading to more lawlessness, even so now present your members as servants to righteousness for holiness" (6:19).

Many instances of such sanctified use of hands are given in the Scriptures. One is the actual physical act of making an oath before God: "And Abram said to the king of Sodom, I have lift up mine hand unto the Lord, the most high God, the possessor of heaven and earth . . ." (Genesis 14:22). The Hebrew for "I have sworn" literally is "I have lifted up my hands." The modern carry-over of taking an oath in civil court is that you "Raise your right hand and repeat after me. . . ."

Moses, you will recall, lifted up his hands (with a bit of help!) in the battle of Israel against the Amalekites (Exodus 17:12). And Solomon lifted up his hands to the Lord, during his prayer of dedication when the temple was consecrated to God (1 Kings 8:22). Both of these uses of hands are obviously related to an appeal to the Lord.

It is out of this background that Paul admonishes in 1 Timothy 2:8, "Therefore I desire that the men pray everywhere, lifting up holy hands, without wrath and doubting."

The lifting up of hands is not a modern "charismatic" phenomenon. Instead, it was an Old Testament practice, carried over into the

New Testament Church. Even to this day, hands are raised throughout the historic Church as the official position for intercessory prayer. How unfortunate that today the use of this position of prayer is limited to the priest or clergyman who is leading the worship. For the whole Church is ". . . a spiritual house, a holy priesthood, to offer up spiritual sacrifices acceptable to God through Jesus Christ" (1 Peter 2:5). In the early centuries of the Church, all the congregation prayed with uplifted hands.

There is another forgotten use of holy hands—forgotten, that is, by some of us moderns in the West. From earliest times, Christian hands traced the sign of the cross across their upper bodies in recognition of the reality of the cross upon which our Lord was crucified. This gesture signaled before the heavenly hosts, before principalities and powers, and before other mortals the continuing efficacy of the work of the Lord Jesus on the cross for us. Though the sign was used by many of our Reformation Fathers, including Martin Luther, it has sadly fallen into disuse in most of Protestantism.

Paul wrote, "God forbid that I should glory except in the cross of our Lord Jesus Christ, by whom the world has been crucified to me, and I to the world" (Galatians 6:14). Many of us are able only to glory in the cross in our minds, or in our imaginations, because we have ceased to do so with our hands. We Protestants have got to get over the delusion that this is a Roman Catholic invention. To the contrary, it is a practice that goes back to at least the second century, and has been employed by "all men everywhere" both in worship and in claiming protection against Satan. Making the sign of the precious cross of our Lord Jesus Christ is not voodoo. It is neither magic nor is it idolatry. It is simply fleshing out with human hands what is true in the heavenlies: that we are redeemed, transformed, and wonderously protected by the cross of Christ. It is an assurance that affirms we are under His Lordship in the same way that we understand God's blessing upon us, when the pastor raises his hand over his people as he gives the benediction.

I am convinced that if we were a bit more free to use hands in our worship of the Father, Son, and Holy Spirit, we would *de facto* protect ourselves from allowing our hands to get into as much mischief as they tend to do.

2. Holy hands are used to reach out for Christ to serve others. Our hands are usually the means by which we perform good works. In Proverbs 31:20 we read of this well-known godly wife and mother, "She stretcheth out her hand to the poor; yea, she reacheth forth her hands to the needy." Face it. Serving others means getting involved, getting our hands dirty for the Lord.

The impact of this truth came home to me forcefully several years ago. An old man, whom we affectionately called "Mr. Fred," came to Christ in our community. A short time later it was my privilege to baptize him. The Lord had spoken to my heart in no uncertain terms and said to me, "He's yours to care for."

As one who had been used to confining most of his ministerial activities to comfortable things, like preaching and teaching, the actual physical care of this poverty-stricken man opened up a whole new vista for me. Through him, I gained a whole new [old] view of Christian ministry. Here was a case where praying with him and teaching him out of the Scriptures were not sufficient. The use of my hands—and my resources—was on the line!

Activities varied all the way from rebuilding a small house for him, to making sure he had warm meals when he was sick as well as providing transportation to the store. Twice a year I drove him out to a neighboring farm and bought him a couple of pigs, which he loved to raise. His death two years ago ended one of the richest and most rewarding eras of my life.

The care of Mr. Fred often demanded many, many hours each week. But, truthfully, I have never known a more delightful responsibility. Through him, I was forced to learn that caring for others is not merely a heart attitude or a willingness to serve; it is actually getting out there and doing it. Through helping him, I experienced firsthand the truth of Jesus' words, "It is more blessed to give than to receive" (Acts 20:35). Part of the reason, I believe, God gave me my own hands was to wait on and serve Mr. Fred.

OUR FEET ARE SET APART TO GOD

As with our hands, we have the same two choices for our feet. There are those whose "feet run to evil" (Proverbs 1:16). Or there are those about whom it is said, "How beautiful upon the mountains are the feet of him that bringeth good tidings ..." (Isaiah 52:7).

Like breathing, or the beating of our hearts, it is easy for us to take the activity of our feet for granted. Their functions are so smoothly coordinated with the rest of our actions that we hardly notice them. While they can be those members of our body which carry us into evil, as the writer of Proverbs so shrewdly observed, King David pointed out a different possibility for the people of God: "I . . . turned my feet unto thy testimonies," and "refrained my feet from every evil way . . ." for "Thy word is a lamp unto my feet, and a light unto my path" (Psalms 119:59, 101, 105). Consequently, the holy woman Hannah could sing, "He will keep the feet of his saints . . ." (1 Samuel 2:9).

Though our feet are used every waking moment, I would like to underscore two reasons God has created us with feet, and how He wants us, as those set apart to Him, to use them.

1. It is our feet which bring us to worship. The psalmist said, "I was glad when they said unto me, Let us go into the house of the Lord" (Psalms 122:1). In Israel of old, you *walked.* And however it is that we come to worship today, ultimately the journey still involves the use of our feet. God gave you two feet to get you from one place to another, to join with others in the Body of Christ to worship Him, to offer Him our spiritual sacrifices.

It is so easy for us in this day and age to forsake "the assembling of ourselves together, as is the manner of some . . ." (Hebrews 10:25). That scriptural admonition is almost prophetic for our times, isn't it? Today, we are told by insinuation, we don't need to "go anywhere to worship God." We can simply pull up a chair in the corner by the lamp and worship Him through reading the Bible and private prayers. Or we can turn on the television and join in with an electronic preacher hundreds of miles down the road.

Reading the Bible is fine. And (depending upon the program) watching something religious on television may be, to a lesser degree, appropriate. But I'll promise you, neither of these activities can ever take the place of the visible Church coming together to worship God.

Recently, I was visiting with a pastor and the subject of a mutual acquaintance—the director of a Christian agency—came up in the conversation. Our concern for the man was that he seemed to have grown cold and spiritually aloof.

"You know, thinking back over the situation," my pastor friend mused, "I think I have a clue to the problem. My wife and I knew this man well in his early days as a Christian. He was part of our Church. He was always there for planning sessions, and took part in almost all of the social activities. But he rarely showed up for worship."

If you or I have problems getting motivated to worship God, we had better go all the way back to where we started with Christ and make sure of our consecration to Him. One of the premier marks of the unholy person is that he is unwilling to give thanks (Romans 1:21). If you cannot bring yourself to worship, it may well be your heart has grown cold—or just lazy. When the people of God only "serve" Him but do not worship Him, that world out there will not be changed.

That our set-apartness to God must find its earthly focus in true worship is absolutely crucial to our understanding of holiness. The place we live out our holiness is, as we have said, in the Body of Christ. The New Testament simply *assumes* that worship is a corporate action, requiring the participation of the whole Church. And the practice of the primitive Christian communities underscores this fact.

Furthermore, the key—the bottom line for all of what being Christian is—is *worship.* We moderns must regain the reality that the worship of God is not a means to an end—*worship is an end in itself.* We are made holy to worship God in spirit and in truth. We do not worship to become more holy. That makes worship a means to an end. We are made holy to worship.

Nor do we worship to get ourselves "charged up" for evangelism. No, evangelism is the means to an end. Understand that evangelism is *not* the most important ministry of the local congregation. Instead, it is *worship.* We evangelize in order to bring men and women to worship the true God. Christ has come to us, and through Him we bring the lost home to the Father that they, too, might worship Him.

There is a lot said today about getting people born again. That's fine, but I'd much prefer to talk of bringing people to Christ. In the former, you make the salvation of the individual the goal; in the latter, Jesus Christ is the goal. Remember, though Jesus Christ came into the world to save sinners (1 Timothy 1:15), at the heart of all He did was His primary objective: to glorify the Father, and to do His will. The Father's aim is for us to worship Him, and through His only-begotten Son, He causes us to be born anew and He sanctifies us in order to do just that.

For me, this helps take care of the "I-didn't-get-anything-out-of-Church-this-morning" mentality. Whoever said *we* are in the Church to get something out of it? That stance makes worship the means to personal fulfillment, which is humanism. I do not go to

Church to "get something out of it." I go to worship God. Granted, when a person gives praise and thanksgiving to God, there are personal blessings; but we do not worship God to receive something. We worship Him to return glory to Him. For worship is an end in itself. And we are made holy to participate in it.

Where is it we go? To Christ. But it is not, as someone has said, "The alone worshiping the Alone." There is a very familiar word we use to describe how we come: we *congregate*. We come as a redeemed family to worship Him. That is why He has made us holy.

So our feet are not simply ours to do with as we want to do. They have been given to us by God; they are set apart unto Him; and they are to be used to bring us to worship the Father, the Son, and the Holy Spirit, in the midst of His holy congregation.

2. Our feet help bring to others the gospel of peace. In his list of Christian armor in Ephesians 6, Paul specifically singles out the feet: "having shod your feet with the preparation of the gospel of peace" (Ephesians 6:15).

The Gospel, as we have stated, is summed up in one sentence: "Repent, for the kingdom of heaven is at hand!" (Matthew 3:2). Our feet are involved in that action, as we participate in calling people to turn around and to be enrolled in the Kingdom of God. The Scriptures do not limit this activity to verbal proclamation only. Without question, verbal witness is involved. Still, we bring the Gospel to others by our wholehearted participation in the warfare of the Kingdom of Light against the kingdom of darkness, and that involves far more than talking. This participation includes acts of service, hospitality, and kindness, as well as contributing a blameless life.

Regardless of how we participate in bringing the "gospel of peace" to others, our activities must include ready feet. And that goes back to our willingness to be used in the first place. Our feet have been given to us by God, not simply to carry out our own wishes, nor to be the contents of a stylish new pair of shoes. They are there to be *used* in bringing the gospel of peace to other people.

OUR MOUTHS ARE SET APART TO GOD

Back at the height of their popularity, the Beatles made a statement which may well have led to the downfall of their career as a rock group. One of them said, "We're more popular than Jesus

Christ." Even the secular press took them to task; a mouth which had sung to the world, now brought wrath down upon itself. The world refused to buy that statement.

Thirty-five hundred years ago, the Lord spoke to Moses and gave him the very basis upon which a holy person views the use of his mouth. In this case, Israel's leader would just as soon have remained anonymous. He was fudging on allowing God the use of his mouth to speak to people. So the Lord asked Moses, ". . . Who hath made man's mouth? or who maketh the dumb, or deaf, or the seeing, or the blind? have not I the Lord? Now therefore go, and I will be with thy mouth, and teach thee what thou shalt say" (Exodus 4:11, 12).

Few of us need to be told of the incredible damage that the wrong use of our mouths can bring. Mouthing off must be a problem common to virtually all of us, for over and over again, from Proverbs through to James, the Scriptures warn against improper use of the tongue. That dangerous little bodily member can produce both blessing and cursing (James 3:10).

Similarly, many positive uses of the mouth are readily apparent to the Christian. We think of bearing witness to Christ, of singing praise to the Lord, of instructing someone in the faith. With these contrasts in mind, I would like to concentrate on two ways in which holy people are able to use their mouths that common men will never know.

1. To give a benediction. By this statement, I am not limiting a benediction to standing up at the end of the worship service, and with a word, sending the people on their way—though that is perhaps the most basic application of the term.

What I have in mind is a more general usage of the term. In its derivation, *benediction* literally means "good word." And what I have in mind is offering words of encouragement, of support, of joy, to those with whom we come in contact, as opposed to being bearers of bad news, gossip, or cruel cuts.

Let us have, then, "good words," which promote strength, love, and unity in the Body of Christ. I believe this use of the mouth is what Paul means when he says, "Let us consider one another so as to stir up love and good works" (Hebrews 10:24).

Nor must we think our manner of response to our enemies is irrelevant. I do not suppose there is a person who has ever drawn a breath who has not been maligned at one point or another by those who harbor hatred and bitterness in their hearts toward him. The natural thing, the "common" thing, is to lash back at these people with our tongues and "get even." But our Lord Jesus gave one of the most valuable pieces of instruction known to men in Matthew 5:44 when He said, "But I say to you, love your enemies, and bless those who curse you. . . ."

What a tremendous passage to remember the next time you are unjustly "nailed" by an adversary. Our natural ("common") response is to lash back when such attacks come. But there is a better way. When the bitterness begins to gurgle in your heart, pray for those involved. When the opportunity comes to meet your accusers face-to-face, follow the Lord's instructions and give them a blessing. For our mouths can be used to speak the good word from God, rather than to spew out any venom, which would be the way of unholiness. And I promise you, being *made* holy is the only way I know to pull this sort of thing off. The inclination of the natural man is just the opposite.

Something else that I've found helpful has to do with my intake of information. I don't know how you feel, but too large a dose of national network evening news brings me into a mood of depression from time to time. I've found that what is taken into my heart and mind will affect what I believe and what I say. Thus, there are days when I, by design, do not read the paper or watch television. I call it a "media fast." Instead, I'll limit my intake on certain days to fellowship with other Christians, the Scriptures, and perhaps a good book. I am amazed at how this affects what comes back out through my mouth!

Only a holy person can give a legitimate blessing or benediction to other people. And how people in our world need those good words! May we be set apart to give them.

2. To receive Communion. After all is said and done, I believe there is no more glorious purpose for God having given us our mouths than to receive the consecrated loaf and cup at the Table of the Lord.

Of all the imaginable uses for the mouth of a holy person, can you think of anything higher, more noble, more dignified than to eat and drink the nourishment that this communion with our Lord and Savior Jesus Christ brings? The mouths of the holy not only give out the praises of God and tell of His benefits, but they also are there to receive the very food of heaven's altar.

And one day, in our glorified state, these resurrected mouths will feast at the Holy Supper of the Lamb, as we dwell in the house of the Lord forever.

A BODY SET APART

Our hands, our feet, our mouths are among the bodily members which God has not only given us by creation, but has redeemed through the blood of Christ and set apart to Himself. We are to be holy through and through, from the top of our heads to the tips of our feet. Being set apart to the Lord involves not only what we are, but what we do as well.

It was in this spirit that Paul wrote these wondrous words of encouragement to the Church at Rome, as found in Romans 12:1, 2:

> I beseech you therefore, brethren, by the mercies of God, that you present your bodies a living sacrifice, holy, acceptable to God, which is your reasonable service.

> And do not be conformed to this world, but be transformed by the renewing of your mind, that you may prove what is that good and acceptable and perfect will of God.

EPILOGUE:

An Open Letter to

Fellow World-Changers

Yes, we want to change the world.

But there must be no confusion about what change we want. We want to see the whole world brought to God the Father and set apart, made holy, to Him. Of course we recognize that not all will turn to Him; perhaps there will only be a small portion. That's all right. We will be glad for whoever turns to Him.

But above all else, we want to be holy people in a holy Church, living as our Father wishes, centered on Him, subjecting everything in our lives to our relationship with Him, and placing our hope and joy in Him. As we have seen, the practical outworking of that relationship means that every aspect of our beings and our lives falls under God's command that we be holy, as He is holy.

The first changes, then, must come in us. We must recognize the absolute sovereignty of Father, Son, and Holy Spirit. That means giving up our independent spirits and actually submitting ourselves to God in His Church. We must actively seek His will for our lives within that context, with and through the aid and direction of duly constituted Church leaders. Right here lies the pill most difficult for modern Americans to swallow, but it must be done if we are to be a holy people. Our "monstrous individualism must go," as C. S. Lewis said regarding himself in *Surprised by Joy*.

Our whole life in Christ, our holiness, is founded upon a joyful acceptance of the Good News of the Incarnation, the humiliation, and the glorification of Christ. If we think of Him simply as God or simply as Man, we lose the distinctive sense of who our Savior is and what He has done for us. This is basic: You will never grow in your walk with Christ, until you learn to adore Him as perfect God and perfect Man in one Person. He is our Savior, because He is God the Word, and He has saved us by truly uniting a complete human nature to His divine nature, "unconfusedly, immutably, indivisibly, inseparably."[16]

This awesome truth is not just a fact to be accepted and digested, however. Indeed, this is the foundation of our faith and the basis upon which we are called to trust in Him for our salvation. To participate in God's plan for changing the world, you must abandon yourself to Christ, throwing yourself upon Him as your only hope. These are not just words to be accepted! Holiness requires whole-hearted trust of Jesus Christ, and actually putting Him *first* in all aspects of life. It is lip service to this sort of consecration, which He called hypocrisy, when He met up with it in the Pharisees.

Serve, as your pastor and other Church leaders call upon you. Be willing to do anything, be it ever so small, to promote the holiness of the Church and its work as the Body of Christ. For too long we evangelical Christians have reserved the right each to decide on his own how, when, and where he will serve. Be willing to be the last and the least!

Join in the prayer of our Lord for the unity of His Church, and work as opportunity arises for its unity in the orthodox faith. Our Lord prayed: "I do not pray for these alone, but also for those who will believe in Me through their word; that they all may be one, even as You, Father, are in Me, and I in You; that they also may be one in Us, that the world may believe that You have sent Me" (John 17:20, 21). Instead of just reading John 17, learn to pray it.

In His prayer, we find the Lord praying that those disciples be consecrated and sanctified. But He didn't mean it just for them. Though He prayed specifically for them, He added, "I do not pray for these alone, but also for those who will believe in Me through their word" (John 17:20). He prayed for all people in every age who were destined to yield to and obey those words, which exhort hearers to receive the sanctification which comes through faith.

This particular prayer has a distinctive object—that *we* may be *one*. He asked the Father that we be brought into a true spiritual unity—a unity so deep and far-reaching, that it will resemble that unity of nature which exists between the Father and the Son.

Admittedly, we do not see such a unity displayed in Christendom today. We have already touched upon that fact. Oh, there is a way in which we are all one: we have all been grafted into Him in and through His glorified humanity, and thus all Christians are one in that we share His humanity. But it will not do to stop there and call that sufficient. As long as we are sectionalized and splintered, we do not have the unity for which He prayed. A divided Church will not make the Jew (Romans 11:14) or anyone else envious. A divided Church lacks the vital elements of holiness.

We are to pray for, long for, and work for, the true and concrete unity of the whole Church. Never mind that it does not seem possible; never mind that there are those who would have us "become one" on a ground which denies our Lord. We trust that *He* will bring about the unity, and *we* simply and prayerfully do that which we are called to do.

Finally, yearn for His coming again. It has been said that we are to live, as if He were coming today, and at the same time—as if He were not coming for another thousand years. We are to expect Him at any time and to be prepared for His imminent return. But we are also to carry on activities in this world, as His people doing His work and planning to do His work.

Doesn't all this sound basic? Old? Normal? If so, you have caught the message. We do not have to be spectacular to please God or to change the world. No—*holy, righteous, obedient, serving,* and *joyful,* will do just fine.

Let us then be a holy, hopeful people, laboring in the world, but not of it, yearning to see Him face-to-face. Let us, to the degree God wills, change the world, but be ever intent on first behaving properly as holy and godly children of our Heavenly Father. And in the end, we shall see Him face-to-face.

Appendix A

A PRIMER ON THE WILL OF GOD

We have concluded that we *can* change the world by becoming a holy and righteous people. Now we are ready to take a good, hard look at God's definition of holy conduct. He first revealed it by His very hand on Mount Sinai thirty-five hundred years ago, in what we know as the Ten Commandments. The Lord Jesus Christ enforced—and strengthened—these commandments in Matthew 5.

(Let me say at the outset that this Appendix is not a dazzling array of glorious new insights. It is incredibly basic—almost vanilla. We are dusting off old foundations for review and for clarity. We are nailing down God's lines of demarcation between right and wrong. So read it in that light!)

THE ROLE OF THE LAW

It is significant to note that God did not give these commands to Israel to make them holy, for keeping even God's Laws cannot make one holy. Only God Himself can make us holy. Nor do we set ourselves apart from common use to belong to the Lord. It is He who performs this work.

God did not start with the Law. *First* He made Israel a holy nation through Abraham. *Then,* through Moses, He told His people how He wanted them to live. He promised they would be His own possession, a special treasure, a *holy nation* unto Him.

Many of us have had the experience of being prospective home buyers, and being shown through a lovely, older home by a real-estate agent. If you're anything like me, while the realtor is trying to explain the benefits and features of the place, I'm busy chatting with my wife: "Let's do that room in a small print wallpaper . . . and what about a chair rail here in the dining room?" But until the house is mine, until it is in my possession, my renovation cannot begin. God first set His people apart as His own; then He called for changes in behavior.

Further, Israel was not to be seen as just *another government* in the world. Instead, God set them apart from all other governments, to be a government of God, a holy government. When the word came from God through Moses that the children of Israel were to be God's chosen race, they responded eagerly, "All that the Lord hath spoken we will do" (Exodus 19:8).

It was at this point, God said, "Consecrate them" (*see* Exodus 19:10). Why? Because, as a nation of people to be set apart to God, they did not simply make themselves holy. Rather, they agreed to be made holy. And then they were *brought into* holiness through consecration—in this case, the washing of their garments (Exodus 19:10). God acted and the people obeyed.

IT'S BOTH-AND

Here, incidentally, the words of Peter to us, "Repent, and . . . be baptized" (Acts 2:38), take on richer meaning. It is never belief *versus* baptism, or willingness *versus* consecration. It is both! We are called upon to willingly commit ourselves to follow Christ; then we are set apart as His holy people.

So the Ten Commandments were given to a people that had been first set apart to the Lord. To repeat: *Keeping the commandments did not make them holy.* If we think keeping the law makes people holy, then we are essentially like the Pharisees and will lapse hopelessly into legalism. Holy people do what God says, but doing what God says does not make them holy.

I have six children who are "set apart" unto me: they are mine. They came to Marilyn and me by birth. Because I am their father and they are my children, we have a specific relationship: we are *family.* In that relationship, they are to do what I say. If they disregard my orders, then in our bond of love we open up some whole new options: discipline, repentance, perhaps restitution, and reconciliation. But we do all this as family. They obey me, because they are my children—not to *become* my children.

Just as I do not tell the neighbors' children what to do, so the Ten Commandments were given to the people of God—God's family—not to the world in general. They are *true* for all men, but they were given to those who were set apart from all other men to be God's holy nation. Paul went so far as to say, in 1 Timothy 1:8–11:

> But we know that the law is good, if one uses it lawfully, knowing this: that the law is not made for a righteous person, but for the lawless and insubordinate, for the ungodly and sin-

ners, for the unholy and profane, for murderers of fathers and murderers of mothers, for manslayers, for fornicators, for sodomites, for kidnappers, for liars, for perjurers, and if there is any other thing contrary to sound doctrine, according to the glorious gospel of the blessed God which was committed to my trust.

We in the family of God have a great advantage over ancient Israel in dealing with the Ten Commandments. At Sinai, the Law of God was written on stone; for the Church, God's Laws are penned by the Holy Spirit on tablets of human hearts (Hebrews 10:16). Under Moses, the Law of God was written *externally* on those tablets of stone. But in Christ, God's Law is inscribed *internally* on human hearts as well.

For the people of Israel, it was, *Here are My commandments written on stone; now do them.* For us who are in Christ, it is, *Here are My commandments written on your hearts, with new power to do them.* The Scriptures teach, "For the law was given by Moses, but grace and truth came by Jesus Christ" (John 1:17).

Thus, the Ten Commandments are God's never-changing revelation of right behavior. His Law is holy, just, and good. It is this same message of righteousness that is written on our hearts by the Holy Spirit, that by His grace, we might do His will.

With morality nearly a bygone in the world, and with right and wrong increasingly fuzzy in the evangelical Church, it is a good time to check back with the infallible written record to make certain that we are properly perceiving the invisible inner deposit of righteousness. How well we know our frightening propensity to become dull of hearing and hardened—going astray in our hearts. Now it is well for us to review what is right and wrong, "... for by the law is the knowledge of sin" (Romans 3:20).

TEN THINGS GOD ABSOLUTELY WANTS YOU TO DO

Here are the holy Laws of God, given with glory to Moses and his people, when Israel had been set apart as a nation for God. They are found in Exodus 20:1–17 based on KJV but couched in modern language. The truth of these Laws comes through to another holy nation, the Church, as it seeks to be soft of heart, to know and obey the will of God.

I. I AM THE LORD YOUR GOD: YOU SHALL HAVE NO OTHER GODS BEFORE ME.

For the humanist, man, his "rights," his interests, are central. For holy people, the One True God is central. As Christians, we are to know and obey the Father, honor His Son Jesus Christ as Lord, and be filled with and led by the Holy Spirit. There is no middle ground.

Being set apart to God means *everything* is under His care. This includes:

My mind and reason. Conscience is not my guide; Christ is. The Lord will work in my conscience to check me when I am out of line, but I do not live by conscience. If conscience guides me, I end up doing whatever is right in my own eyes (compare with Judges 21:25). Instead, the Lord Jesus Christ is my guide.

My future is in God's hands, for I "walk by faith, not by sight" (2 Corinthians 5:7). My plans, dreams, and aspirations all come under God's scrutiny and are subject to His will.

My money and possessions are the Lord's. I am merely the caretaker or steward of His possessions, for ". . . all things were created by Him and for Him" (Colossians 1:16).

My identity is determined by Him. In the old covenant, the believer had his identity in Israel. Under the new covenant, our identity is in the Church, the Body of Christ. The First Commandment is not simply God talking to the individual. It is God addressing His holy nation, with whom each Israelite was identified. Similarly, Christ is not privately my head or privately your head. He is the glorious Head of the Church, of which we who believe are part.

Every now and then, you will hear a pseudopious individualist declare religiously, "My relationship with Jesus comes ahead of the Church." That would be like a confused wife saying, "My relationship with my husband comes ahead of our marriage." As members of the Bride of Christ, it is our union with Him in His Body that secures His reign over us as Lord. Our identity with Christ is in His Church, not separate from it. For the Church is that place where we are set apart from that which is common in the world.

II. YOU SHALL NOT MAKE FOR YOURSELF AN IDOL (OR ANY LIKENESS OF WHAT IS IN HEAVEN ABOVE OR ON THE EARTH BENEATH). YOU SHALL NOT WORSHIP NOR SERVE SUCH IDOLS.

The Second Commandment warns us to worship nothing but the true God who has revealed Himself. In our culture there are two extremes of idolatry that we must especially guard against: (1) the political or economic state, and (2) the individual.

The political or economic state. For some who say they are Christians, preoccupation with politics supersedes commitment to Christ and His Church. They may claim otherwise, but their actions belie their words. And it happens to both liberals and conservatives.

Remember the Eugene McCarthy/George McGovern devotees? They were convinced that both men were political deliverers; these two candidates held the answers for the USA. Neither man was elected president, and somehow, the nation survived and the world kept spinning.

Then along came a string of born-again candidates. (Note how easy it has gotten of late to be born again!) There was Nixon, Ford, Carter, Reagan, all of whom eventually held the highest office in the land. But none has held the ultimate solutions, nor was any one of them really supposed to. There is just one Messiah, and none other will ever come forward to take His place. To say or to hope otherwise is idolatry.

Big business, the *corporation,* can also become an idol. And, again, it can trap both labor and management. People of God, free enterprise or "getting mine" is not our salvation. I happen to like our economic system, but it cannot become our lord or success our ultimate priority. Only the government and economy of God will prevail. That is where my loyalty must lie.

The individual. For others (and ironically for some of the same people who commit to secular politics and economics), individual liberty becomes preeminent. Phrases like *personal choice* or *self-determination* or *individual freedom* are seen as sacred. I appreciate the personal liberty I have, but it is by no means my passion. For just as the secular or corporate state is not my ultimate, neither is personal determinism. Far, far more precious is the reality that Jesus Christ is Lord, and that I am accountable to Him in His Church. In my commitment to Him and His people, I stand a decent, fighting chance to be saved from political or personal idolatry.

Images. While we are on the subject of idolatry, let us address a final problem. A small minority of religious people in the last several centuries have misconstrued this Second Commandment to teach that no imagery whatever is appropriate for Christian use. Such sects scoff at the cross atop a church building, disdain Christian art, and ridicule any enhancement of worship.

Is such an interpretation of this command correct? No, it is not. Remember, Israel was instructed, *after* the Second Commandment was given, to construct an earthly tabernacle and later the temple. These were to be "the copy and shadow of the heavenly things" (Hebrews 8:5). The celestial tabernacle was God's pattern for the earthly structure. There is a heavenly mercy-seat, and an earthly one; there are heavenly cherubim, and there are earthly renderings. There are proper holy images and there are unholy or *graven* images. The former have the blessing of God; the latter are condemned by Him as idols, things we have made for ourselves.

From the beginning, the cross has been a universal symbol of the work of Christ on behalf of the Church. We wear the cross around our necks; it is imprinted on our Bibles; it is engraved on the Table of the Lord. We do not worship the cross. Instead, we worship and adore Him who upon the cross was sacrificed for our sins and who arose on the third day.

Even the Bible itself, the inspired written record of God's revelation, is also used as imagery in the Church. It is printed on the best paper, with the finest ink, embossed with gold and bound with the most precious leathers. In the councils of the ancient Church, an open Bible was placed in the middle of the room, that all might remember the standard by which decisions would be made. To this day, open Bibles grace the altars and lecterns of the church as constant reminders of the truth of the Gospel.

Long before the final canonization of the Scriptures, there appeared in the Churches images, *icons,* of Christ and His holy ones. Interestingly, these were never painted with great realism. The idea was that the icon should remind us of the age to come and of men who have been regenerated into that heavenly realm. It was the *person* who was to be honored, not the picture. Whether our picture of Christ be that of Sallman, or Hook, or an ancient iconographer, we reserve our worship for the Person of Christ alone.

And as pictures of my Christian grandparents, as well as pictures of saints Paul and Athanasius are displayed on my bedroom wall, it is the persons depicted, not the pictures themselves, to whom I give honor.

All of us bow ultimately to something or someone. Holy men and women do not stake their lives on governments, businesses, or individuals—themselves included. Their trust is in Christ through His Church.

III. YOU SHALL NOT TAKE THE NAME OF THE LORD YOUR GOD IN VAIN.

The names of the Father, the Son, and the Holy Spirit are, as we have noted, *holy* names. Of Jesus Christ we read, ". . . there is no other name under heaven given among men by which we must be saved" (Acts 4:12). Of the Father, Jesus said, "I have declared to them Your name . . ." (John 17:26). And blaspheming the name of the Holy Spirit is unforgivable.

Have you ever heard people say, "Mohammed dammit" or "Buddha Almighty!"? Why not? Because their gods are powerless, dead, and in their graves. Our God inhabited human flesh, was crucified, and is alive from the dead, seated in the heavenlies. The very mention of **JESUS CHRIST** holds a certain power and majesty. Walk into a room and mention Confucius or Zoroaster or Lao-tzu, and nothing much happens. But begin talking about Jesus Christ and temperatures rise; people are offended and disturbed. Holy ones are blessed.

Isaiah tells us His name is Wonderful. We who are set apart to Him are to keep His name holy.

In our day, protecting the name of the Lord has further ramifications. Vows in the courtroom ("so help me God") are to be kept. So are the vows of marriage. When a man and woman stand before the Lord and give themselves to one another "in the name of the Father, Son, and Holy Spirit," that oath is for *keeps*. To violate that union with divorce reduces marriage to the profane, the common.

The humanist looks for a way out. "My needs aren't met," he alleges, or, "We are not compatible." The righteous say, "God gives us grace in marriage; we made a promise in His Name, and we will love one another just as we promised, 'for better or for worse.' " In Christian marriage, we take our hands off the back doorknob. With the help of God we keep our word. For we have been made holy and have been given His power to live righteously. We do not profane His name.

IV. REMEMBER THE SABBATH DAY, TO KEEP IT HOLY.

I went through a period in my life some years back that has been called "superspirituality"—which, in reality, is no spirituality at all. It's that attitude which says *every* day is a day for worship; therefore we will treat Sunday as all other days. Let me say it categorically: When you try to make every day a "sabbath," it absolutely backfires. You end up with *no* Lord's Day. Every day becomes common. And this is what has happened in the secular world, and even among some Christians.

In the Law, God set aside a special day each week for His people to *worship Him* and *rest.* In the old covenant this was the seventh day. Our Lord Jesus Christ established the first day of the week as the day when His holy people, the Church, would specifically draw aside from their work to worship Him. Under the new covenant, the Church, for two thousand years, has in every place honored Sunday, Resurrection Day, as the Lord's day.

In our time, Sunday is a business-as-usual day, just like the other six. But the saints of God put aside their secular work, turn to the Lord in thanksgiving with His congregation, and refresh their minds and bodies with a break from the routine of the week. Worship is a change of pace called rest.

How much work do you and I refrain from? As much as possible. For the Christian, the issue in all things is not how much can we get away with and still be called holy. Instead, it is to see how obedient we can be to the Lord of life. Let the world work, if it wants to. For me, Sunday is a holy day, a day for worship. It is not mine to redefine or grab back for myself.

V. HONOR YOUR FATHER AND YOUR MOTHER, THAT YOUR DAYS MAY BE LENGTHENED IN THE LAND WHICH THE LORD YOUR GOD GIVES YOU.

This command to honor parents is the first one with a promise: "that it may be well with you and you may live long on the earth" (Ephesians 6:3). I believe this includes both our physical and our spiritual parents.

To honor our parents means to obey them. It means to treat them with respect and to speak well of them to other people.

Later in life, when we are out from under our parents' roof, we still are called to honor them. As an adult you may go in a different direction from that of your parents—particularly if you are Christian, and they are not. Even so, we are responsible before God to treat our parents with dignity and respect all of our lives. Maintain contact with your parents. Write them and phone them, and keep them informed of the progress of your life and the lives of their grandchildren. Make every effort to assure that they are taken care of and are content.

Similarly, we honor our Fathers and Mothers in the Church. The last verse of the Old Testament is: "And he shall turn the heart of the fathers to the children, and the heart of the children to their fathers, lest I come and smite the earth with a curse" (Malachi 4:6).

I believe this word is prophetic for us in our day. I sense the Holy Spirit is impressing upon Christian people—as He did during the days of the Reformation—that it is time to return to the faith of the Fathers. We are to honor those godly ones who have gone before us in the Church. In fact, the Scripture calls us to give our elders double honor (1 Timothy 5:17).

VI. YOU SHALL NOT MURDER.

Holy people do not take someone else's life—or their own. Because it is God who gives life, and makes man in His image, there is a *sanctity* of human life. It is He who determines its bounds.

Jesus said, in Matthew 5:21, 22:

> You have heard that it was said to those of old, "You shall not commit murder," and whoever murders will be in danger of the judgment.

> But I say to you that whoever is angry with his brother without a cause will be in danger of the judgment. And whoever says to his brother, *"Raca!"* will be in danger of the council. But whoever says, "You fool!" will be in danger of hell fire.

In the Church we are to stay reconciled with each other to keep enmities and hatred from building up. Holy people love their enemies—that means people out in the world—and pray for them (Matthew 5:44). We cannot afford the luxury of bitterness. Christians living in hatred, within the Church or outside her, keep the world from being salted and enlightened.

A popular, almost chic, form of murder in our day is the killing of unborn human persons. Over 9 million preborn people were murdered in the USA in the "Me" decade of the seventies under a banner called "abortion on demand." Tearing unborn children from their mothers' wombs is unholy. I believe that unless guilty parents and medical personnel involved in this sin bow down in true sorrow before God and repent, they will face the danger of eternal judgment. Distinguish for me the difference between 6 million Jews, choked to death in Hitler's gas chambers, and over 9 million unborn infants, lying dead in plastic liners of medical clinic trash cans.

Where I live in California, more uproar comes when someone cuts down a tree or runs over a dog, than when a child is aborted. Recently in San Francisco a woman died, and her will ordered that her dog be put to sleep upon her death, rather than being left lonely and neglected. Three thousand petitions came in from people across the country, asking the dog be spared. California lawmakers passed an emergency bill to save the dog, which was signed by the governor the night before the Superior Court Judge heard the case.

The next day the courtroom was packed, as the judge was called out to take the call notifying him that the governor had signed the bill. Onlookers applauded with delight, as the decision to spare the dog was read. The story made international news.

Personally, I like animals, and I am glad the dog's life was saved. But the logic of mobilizing the government of an entire state and the sentiments of a whole nation to spare a dog—while on the same day countless unborn babies were murdered under the protection of the same judicial system—is, to me, incomprehensible.

Our generation has also seen the rise of another form of murder: euthanasia. This is the premature ending of life for those who are dying from old age or disease. Some doctors, public health officials, and hospitals are now supporting such killing.

And suicide is back in vogue. In Western Europe, a new prosuicide fad has appeared which is fast invading this country as well. Face it: You will know times of depression and despair in your lifetime. It is often in these hours of darkness that Satan tempts, even a child of God, to take his own life, to destroy something God has created. The Scriptures say, "... Resist the devil and he will flee from you" (James 4:7). Suicide in any form is sin. It is never an option for a Christian. It is murder in just another one of its many forms.

One last comment on this commandment. When someone over-works, overeats, or burns the candle at both ends, he may rightly hear a friend say, "You're killing yourself!" We are, if we fail to take care of ourselves and protect the gift of life we have been given by God. As Christians, our bodies are temples of the Holy Spirit, especially precious commodities, which are set apart unto God. What is holy must be treated with sacred trust.

VII. YOU SHALL NOT COMMIT ADULTERY.

Holy people are commanded to be faithful in the sexual union of marriage. If single, they are to live in sexual purity.

Some time ago, I was invited to give a series of sermons in a large church in the Southeast. After the Sunday worship, an older man approached me and asked to talk privately. We walked out to the parking lot to visit.

"All I want from you is a *yes* or *no* answer," he said. "I've talked to other people about my problem, and nobody will give me a firm reply. I'm sixty-five, my wife died several years ago, and I'm lonely. There is a lady down the street who is a widow, also living alone. We have been having sexual relations together for some time. She says God wants our needs met. What I want you to tell me—yes or no—is this sin or is it not?"

I was a bit startled by his directness, and by his obvious sincerity in asking this question. "It is sin," I said.

"Thank you. That's all I needed to know," he replied.

Scripture plainly teaches us:

> Marriage is honorable among all, and the bed undefiled; but fornicators and adulterers God will judge.   Hebrews 13:4

> For this you know, that no fornicator, unclean person, nor cov-etous man, who is an idolater, has any inheritance in the king-dom of Christ and God.   Ephesians 5:5

In our era, the implication is that even single people have got to be having sex to be normal. What a lie! It's time for the people of God to take control over their sexual passions, instead of being controlled by them. When temptation comes we are to say, "Lord, I will to follow you—not my fleshly desires. I am saying *no* this instant to my desire."

Personally, I find immeasurable freedom in avoiding things designed to motivate sexual sin, such as "skin flicks," sensual literature, and loose friends. Bad company *does* corrupt good morals.

And permit me to say a brief word to fellow Christian leaders and pastors. Brethren, divorce is ripping our ranks to shreds. Not only are we making ourselves the laughingstock of those who oppose the faith, but far more seriously, we are making a mockery out of the holiness of God. If you are having difficulties in your marriage, or with resisting desires to commit adultery, I beg you to go to your superior, or to a neighboring pastor, and submit to his guidance for ministry and correction. If you have left your wife for another woman, and swept the matter under the rug, swallow your pride and self-image, and repent for your sin before God and your people. To deny it will invite further judgment and cause untold stumbling to other precious people who may be struggling with this same crisis themselves.

VIII. YOU SHALL NOT STEAL.

The ramifications of this commandment go far beyond exhorting holy people not to be thieves. We who are set apart from commonness are to:

- pay off our debts when they are due;
- respect other people's property by replacing things we damage;
- be honest and up front with our customers in business when it comes to selling our products;
- give the boss an honest day's work, even if we feel he is too harsh, demanding, or unjust;
- pay a decent and just wage to those who work for us, thereby taking an active role in standing against poverty;
- use energy carefully and unselfishly;
- treat the creation with utmost respect and care.

In the USA economic system, we have been allotted a great measure of personal liberty, as compared with the rest of the world. It is *so* easy to lapse into making the gain of temporal things our primary motivation. Christians often forget they work for God first. Too many live to make a buck, impress the boss, or beat the system.

If God has really set us apart to Himself, then let's go ahead and pay our taxes gratefully, come to work early now and then, and serve others with gladness. We have been removed from the commonness of greed and dishonest gain to serve the living God—and be thankful. I think the world is waiting to see a generation of Christian business people in whom they can safely trust.

IX. YOU SHALL NOT BEAR FALSE WITNESS AGAINST YOUR NEIGHBOR.

As members of Christ, we are to love the truth and hate what is evil—not participating in lying, deceit, or slander. Such things come from Satan, "a liar and the father of it" (John 8:44). The first bishop of Jerusalem writes: "If anyone among you thinks he is religious, and does not bridle his tongue but deceives his own heart, this one's religion is useless" (James 1:26).

Gossip has always been a cancerous seed sown by the enemy among the people of God. As holy men and women, let us reject malicious tales the moment they appear. We are not to be purveyors of lies about others. In the Church, we are to speak well of fellow saints. "Therefore let us pursue the things which make for peace and the things by which one may edify another" (Romans 14:19).

Conversely, this command does not preclude us bearing a true witness against a fellow saint, should there be legitimate cause. In that case, we speak the truth *in love*. But we must take care to not exaggerate or stretch the truth. It is so natural, so *common*, to make things better or worse than they really are.

I have great concern over the way Christian agencies embellish reports of their spiritual results to constituents. We read about "multiplied thousands" of decisions here, "entire cities shaken" there. Beloved, if these things are not really true, they are lies. Do not report them.

And can't we tell of our failures, too, to make the picture an honest one? Luke did in the Book of Acts. How about those who came to Christ and apostatized after a time? Or those who *weren't* healed after we had prayed? Beloved, we are called to be evangelistic, not "evange*last*ic."

X. YOU SHALL NOT COVET.

This command includes not coveting our neighbor's house, wife, servants, beast of burden (in our day, car?) or anything that belongs to him.

There is a certain mystique in items which are not ours. The world calls it "keeping up with the Joneses." So what if the grass is greener on the other side of the fence? Coveting is sin, and succumbing to it dishonors God.

It is helpful for all of us to recognize that others will excel us in what we do. There is a popular notion abroad that "all men are created equal." True, God loves all His people equally; all are equally precious in His sight. All men are not, however, *created* equal. The fact is, some people are smarter, better looking, more intelligent, and more gifted than others. The parable of the talents tells us this. We are thus to be content with what we have.

The Scripture says, " . . . if one member [of the Church] is honored, all the members rejoice with it" (1 Corinthians 12:26). This means if Charlie gets a raise, you are honored, too. If Susie gets an *A,* cheer her on. If Fred can afford a new car, praise God for it.

Jesus promised, "But seek first the kingdom of God and His righteousness, and all these things will be added to you" (Matthew 6:33). What a freedom not to have to want other people's *things!* God will see to it we have what we need.

In Psalms 19:7 we read, "The law of the Lord is perfect. . . ." In that Law the holiness of God is revealed, and in it we see with vivid clarity that He has high standards of conduct for His set-apart people. These standards are sobering, far higher than any rule of life human beings would be willing to set for themselves.

Nevertheless, when our Lord Jesus Christ appeared on earth at the time of His Incarnation, He strengthened rather than weakened them! But with His demands, He offers us His matchless power. He has given us provisions to make righteousness a reality.

Appendix B

In February 1839, Julius Hare preached a sermon to students at the University of Cambridge, in which he extended the list of Hebrews 11 through New Testament days and on to his own. I can think of no more appropriate appendix to chapter 5, "Crossing the Line," than his historical summary of faith in the Church. "The Cloud of Witnesses" is also a fitting conclusion to this book.

By Faith the first believers sold their possessions and goods, and had all things common.

By Faith the Apostles rejoiced that they were counted worthy to suffer for the name of Christ.

By Faith Stephen saw the heavens opened, and the Son of Man standing on the right hand of God. By Faith, when stoned, he fell asleep, praying that God would not lay the sin of his death to the charge of his murderers.

By Faith Peter received the Gentiles into the Church.

By Faith Paul called the nations to the knowledge of Christ. By Faith he founded Church after Church, whithersoever he went. By Faith he stood before Felix, and Festus, and Agrippa. By Faith he was in labours more abundant, in stripes above measure, in prisons more frequent, in deaths oft. By Faith he gloried in the things which concerned his infirmities. By Faith, being carried in bonds to Rome, he turned his captivity into the means of enlarging and strengthening the empire of Christ. By Faith he forgot the things that were behind, and, reaching forward to the things that were before, ever pressed toward the mark, for the prize of the high calling of God in Christ Jesus. By Faith he desired to depart and to be with Christ. By Faith he was content to remain for the furtherance and joy of our Faith.

By Faith the glorious company of the Apostles sealed their testimony in behalf of their crucified Lord with their blood.

By Faith the Son of Thunder, who desired to call down fire on the Samaritan village, became the Apostle of love. By Faith he sought out the backsliding convert amid his band of robbers, and brought him back to the obedience of the Gospel. By Faith when too feeble to walk, and scarcely able to speak, he still bade his friends carry him daily into the midst of the congregation, and said again and again, "Little children, love one another."

By Faith Polycarp, when above ninety years old, being commanded to revile Christ, with the promise that he should be set free, replied, "Eighty and six years have I served Him; and He has done me no wrong. How can I blaspheme my King, who has saved me?" By Faith, as the executioners were about to nail him to the stake, he said, "Leave me as I am: for he who ordains that I should endure the fire, will enable me to stand unflinchingly at the pile, without your nails to hold me." By Faith while they were kindling the fire, he prayed: "O Father of Thy beloved and blessed Son Jesus Christ, through whom I have received the knowledge of Thee, O God of angels and powers, and of the whole creation, and of the whole family of the just who live before Thee, I bless Thee that Thou hast thought me worthy of this day and hour, to obtain a portion among the martyrs, in the cup of Christ, for the resurrection both of soul and body to eternal life, in the incorruptibleness of the Holy Spirit. Therefore, and for all things, I praise Thee, I bless Thee, I glorify Thee, through the eternal High Priest Jesus Christ, Thy beloved Son; through whom be glory to Thee along with Him in the Holy Spirit, both now and through all future ages. Amen."

By Faith thousands of weak frail mortals, even women, felt their hearts glow with joy, when they heard the rabble in their blood-thirsty frenzy cry, "The Christians to the lions!"—the exultation of the victims triumphing over that of the murderers.

By Faith the blood of the martyrs became the seed of the Church.

By Faith the persecuted Christians, in time of terrible pestilence and famine, alone tended and nursed their persecutors, buried them when they died, and calling the people together distributed bread amongst them; whereby the people were moved to glorify Him, whose servants showed such love to their enemies.

By Faith the Syrian hermit, Telemachus, came from the far East to Rome, and, resolving to stop the gladiatorial contests, rushed into the middle of the amphitheatre, and threw himself between the combatants: whereupon, though he was slain by the fury of the populace, yet the horror excited by the act, and the admiration of his self-devotion, brought about the abolition of those games, which the emperors had been unable to suppress.

By Faith Ambrose preserved the churches of Milan from the

Arian empress and her Gothic soldiers. By Faith, making use of rebukes and warnings and threats, he withheld Valentinian from sacrificing to idols. By Faith he forbade the bloodstained Theodosius to approach the altar, until as he had followed David in his crime, he had also followed David in his penitence; whereby the emperor was moved to an earnest and lasting repentance.

By Faith Chrysostom, when deposed, an aged exile in a remote savage land, assailed by all manner of sufferings, still watched over, exhorted, and comforted, his church at Constantinople, still laboured for extending the kingdom of Christ among the heathens, and died with the words he was ever repeating on his lips, "Glory be to God for all things!"

By Faith Athanasius, during forty years of persecution, in banishment time after time, upheld the true doctrine of the Holy Trinity against the power of the emperors, and was the chief human means whereby that doctrine was received and acknowledged as the central truth of the Catholic Church.

By Faith Gregory, when he saw the captive Angels, exclaimed that, were it only for their beauty, they ought to be received into the brotherhood of the angels, and sent Augustin to preach the Gospel in this land.

By Faith Boniface, leaving his home, and refusing high ecclesiastical honours, went forth into the wilds of Germany, to convert the heathen natives. By Faith he cut down the huge oak of Thor, while the people were raging tumultuously around, expecting that the vengeance of the god would burst upon his head. By Faith he built a church to the true God, out of the oak he had cut down, and persuaded the people to worship there. By Faith he baptised above a hundred thousand souls in the name of the Holy Trinity, and built many churches and convents in dreary savage lands. By Faith, when placed at the head of the German Church, he still, in his seventy-fifth year, persevered in enlarging the kingdom of Christ, went forth to convert fresh heathen tribes, and met his martyrdom with patient joy.

By Faith the Hermit Peter and Bernard stirred up the nations of Europe to march as one man, kings and princes and lords, with their assembled vassals, to deliver the birthplace and tomb of the Savior from the unbeliever.

By Faith Bonaventura, being asked in what books he had learned marvellous wisdom, pointed to his crucifix.

By Faith Elizabeth of Hungary, the daughter of kings, the wife of the Duke of Thuringia, being left a widow at twenty, gave all she had to the poor, and dwelt amongst them as their servant, labouring for them, visiting them, waiting upon them, nursing them, by word and deed teaching them the love of God.

By Faith the Waldensians retired among mountain fastnesses, and dwelt in the caves of the Alps, that they might preserve their religion in undefiled purity; and thus have been enabled to preserve it, like the snows around them, under all manner of persecution, through six centuries—a period seldom vouchsafed to the glory of anything earthly.

By Faith Wicliff, the morning-star of the Reformation, rose out of the darkness, and heralded the coming daylight.

By Faith Luther proclaimed his Theses against the doctrine of Indulgences. By Faith he burned the Pope's Bull, and thereby for himself and for millions and millions after him threw off the crushing yoke of Rome. By Faith he went to the diet at Worms, though warned that the fate of Huss would await him, going, as he said, in the strength of Christ, despite the gates of hell, and of the prince of the powers of the air. By Faith a single friendless monk, standing before the princes of the Empire, he witnessed a noble confession with meekness in behalf of the truth. By Faith he translated the Bible and received the glorious reward of being the interpreter of the word of God to his countrymen for all generations.

By Faith Rogers, the protomartyr of our Reformation, when his wife and his eleven children met him on his way to the stake, and an offer of life and pardon was brought to him in their sight, if so be he would recant, walked on with a stout heart, and washed his hands in the flames while he was burning, rejoicing in the fiery baptism whereby he gave up his soul to God.

By Faith Ridley looked forward with joy to the fire that awaited him, and bade his sister come to his marriage.

By Faith the aged Latimer, when stripped to his shroud, rose up on high, as though his very body had been new-strung, and cheered his own heart, and his companion's, by the prophetic assurance, that they should on that day by God's grace light such a candle in England, as would never be put out.

By Faith the noble army of martyrs mounted in their fiery chariots to heaven.

By Faith Oberlin went forth among the Vosges, and labouring in all things at the head of his people spread the blessings of religion and civilization among the wild inhabitants.

By Faith Clarkson and Wilberforce overthrew the slave-trade: and as it is the nature of the grain of mustard-seed to grow until it has become great among the trees of the forest, so through their Faith has slavery been already abolished throughout the British dominions. . . .

And what shall I say more? For the time would fail me to tell of Ignatius, and Justin, and Cyprian, and Perpetus, and Basil, and Augustin, and Patrick, and Columban, and Bede . . . and Melanchton . . . and Francis Xavier, who by Faith subdued kingdoms for Christ, wrought righteousness, obtained the fulfillment of the promises, stopped the mouths of blasphemers, and filled them with hymns of praise, quenched the violence of hatred, melting it into love, out of weakness were made strong, waxed valiant in the fight against Satan, and turned armies of aliens to bow before the name of the living God.

Women and maidens withstood the entreaties of their parents and children, looking with longing for the moment that was to open the gates of immortality. Children rejoiced in the thought of the glorious city to which they were going. Others, thousands upon thousands, devoted their lives to the humblest labours in the service of Him, whom they would gladly have glorified by their deaths.

Wherefore, seeing, brethren, that we also are compassed about with so great a Cloud of Witnesses, let us lay aside every weight, and our besetting sin, and let us run the race set before us with patience, looking to Jesus the Author and Finisher of our Faith.

Julius Charles Hare, *The Victory of Faith and Other Sermons* (London: Griffith Farren Okeden and Welsh, 1840).

Source Notes

Chapter 2
1. The idea for this story is not mine. It is from a sermon by an evangelical Lutheran pastor on the West Coast, given several years ago. I cannot credit the source.

Chapter 4
2. S. B. Shaw, *Dying Testimonies of Saved and Unsaved*, no date, no publisher, p. 180.

Chapter 5
3. Frances Eastwood, *Marcella of Rome* (New York: Dodd & Mead, Publishers, 1870), pp. 5, 6.

Chapter 6
4. It is fair for us to note that biblical baptism is disturbing to a small percentage of people in Christendom today who feel it may open the door to a "works salvation." Let me answer this matter with two brief statements: (1) God commands we be baptized into Christ; and (2) we do not baptize ourselves. We *receive* baptism. This is the precious doctrine of salvation by grace through faith. Baptism is the God-ordained conduit of that grace, just as wire cable is the conduit of generated electric current. The *source* of new life is God; the *means* through which union with Christ comes is in Holy Baptism.
5. The question really boils down to this: Is the flesh of Christ life-giving or is it not? If it is not, then all of us, from the most rabid sign-and-symbolist to the most vociferous sacramentalist, might as well pack up our bags and forget salvation altogether. But, if His flesh is life-giving, which the Scriptures say it is, then it is time to ask the second question: How do we receive life from His flesh? For the answer, we turn to the very words of Jesus Christ Himself in John 6:53–56.
6. Unpublished paraphrase of Saint Cyril's commentary, by Jack N. Sparks.

Chapter 7
7. Vincent of Lerins, *Commonitories,* translated by Rudolf E. Morris (New York: Fathers of the Church, Inc., 1949) pp. 270, 271.
8. Saint John Chrysostom, *Commentary on Saint John the Apostle and Evangelist,* Homilies 48–88. Fathers of the Church, Vol. 41 (Washington, D.C.: The Catholic University of America Press, 1959), p. 189.

Chapter 8

9. G. A. Williamson, translator, *Eusebius: The History of the Church From Christ to Constantine* (Minneapolis: Augsburg Publishing House, 1965), pp. 72, 99–103.

10. Jack N. Sparks, editor, *Apostolic Fathers* (Nashville: Thomas Nelson, Inc., 1978), p. 78.

11. Walter J. Chantry, *God's Righteous Kingdom* (Carlisle, Pennsylvania: The Banner of Truth Trust, 1980), pp. 193, 194.

Chapter 9

12. Saint Athanasius, *Resurrection Letters,* paraphrased and edited by Jack N. Sparks (Nashville: Thomas Nelson, Inc., 1979), p. 90.

13. St. Augustine's Commentary on Psalm 111.

14. *Ecclesiastical Polity*, Book VLXXI (New York: Dutton, Everyman's Library, No. 202), pp. 372, 373.

15. This phrase is used repeatedly in the Easter Service Liturgy of the Orthodox Church, found in the *Service Book of the Holy Orthodox Catholic and Apostolic Church* by Isabel Florence Hapgood (Englewood, New Jersey: Antiochian Orthodox Church, Archdiocese of New York, and all North America, 1975).

Epilogue

16. "The Definition of Faith of the Council of Chalcedon, The Seven Ecumenical Councils," *Nicene and Post Nicene Fathers,* standard series, vol. 14 (Grand Rapids: Wm. B. Eerdmanns Sons), pp. 264, 265.